"A brilliant 'splice of life' from a visionary teacher and editor. Pepperman challenges the routine and cliché by offering a new and vivid conversation about the art of film editing."

> — Joan Brooker
> Director of the award-winning documentary *We Got Us*

"An inspirational guide for editors. Richard's book transports me back to his class — a nice place to be."

> — Núria Olivé-Bellés, Director/Editor
> Official Selections: Montreal, Max Ophuls & Sitges Film Festivals

"Pepperman not only shares his knowledge of editing's art and craft, he gives wholly of himself — insights, philosophies, humor, and risks of being fully alive to seeing and feeling. To study with Richard is a privilege; to read this book is to receive a profound gift."

> — Louis Phillips
> Playwright, author of *The Last of the Marx Brothers' Writers*

"A distinctive approach to the education of all those wanting to understand visual structure. It all makes sense!"

> — Salvatore Petrosino
> Director of Operations
> Film Department, School of Visual Arts

"Pepperman brings decades of experience as an editor and teacher to lessons supported by example and illustration. Here is a voice that is caring and supportive. [To read] *The Eye Is Quicker* is [to attend] a master class."

> — Vincent LoBrutto
> Author of *Selected Takes; Kubrick: A Biography*

"The qualities that have made Richard so inspiring and beloved a teacher — passion, curiosity, humor, and humility — make this book as alive and enticing as a class or conversation with him. *The Eye Is Quicker* will benefit future generations of film editors. It is a very good read for film lovers, and a rich mine for practitioners in the other arts."

> — Jennifer Dunning
> *The New York Times*

"Pepperman goes beyond the mechanical rules of cutting to help us better understand the filmmaking process. *The Eye Is Quicker* increased my awareness of the Shot/Actor/Audience relationship."

> — Igor Sunara
> Director of Photography, *The Keeper*
> (Official Entry: Sundance Festival)

"A highly informative book — stimulating material."

> — Chris Newman
> Three-time Academy Award-winning Production Sound Mixer

"Pepperman's clarity and insight are unsurpassed, and contagious. Years of experience and wisdom [have brought] this monumental book to fruition. *The Eye Is Quicker* should be read by all in the industry."

> — Leonard Lionnet, D.M.A.
> Composer & Member of the Academy of Television Arts & Sciences
> Honored for outstanding work in international television

"No one has Pepperman's perspective on film editing."

> — Everett Aison
> Screenwriter
> Co-Founder, School of Visual Arts Film School

MICHAEL WIESE PRODUCTIONS
www.mwp.com

We are delighted that you have found, and are enjoying, our books.

Since 1981, we've been all about providing filmmakers with the very best information on the craft of filmmaking: from screenwriting to funding, from directing to camera, acting, editing, distribution, and new media.

It is our goal to inspire and empower a generation (or two) of film and video-makers like yourself. But we want to go beyond providing you with just the basics. We want to shake you and inspire you to reach for your dreams and go beyond what's been done before. Most films that come out each year waste our time and enslave our imaginations. We want to give you the confidence to create from your authentic center, to bring something from your own experience that will truly inspire others and bring humanity to its full potential — avoiding those urges to manufacture derivative work in order to be accepted.

Movies, television, the Internet, and new media all have incredible power to transform. As you prepare your next project, know that it is in your hands to choose to create something magnificent and enduring for generations to come.

This is not an impossible goal because you've got a little help. Our authors are some of the most creative mentors in the business, willing to share their hard-earned insights with you. Their books will point you in the right direction but, ultimately, it's up to you to seek that authentic something on which to spend your precious time.

We applaud your efforts and are here to support you. Let us hear from you.

Sincerely,

Michael Wiese
Filmmaker, Publisher

the eye is quicker

film editing: making a good film better   richard d. pepperman

Published by Michael Wiese Productions
11288 Ventura Blvd, Suite 621
Studio City CA 91604
Tel. (818) 379-8799
Fax (818) 986-3408
mw@mwp.com
www.mwp.com

Cover Design: agdesign.com
Layout: Gina Mansfield
Editor: Paul Norlen

Printed by Sheridan Books, Ann Arbor, Michigan
Manufactured in the United States of America

Library of Congress Cataloging-in-Publication Data

Pepperman, Richard D., 1942-
   The eye is quicker : film editing : making a good film better / by
Richard D. Pepperman.
      p. cm.
   ISBN 0-941188-84-1
   1. Motion pictures–Editing. I. Title.
TR899 .P465 2004
778.5'35–dc22

                                                          2003021825

for
Melvin & Ruth Miller

table of contents

I'm concerned that the tradition of passing on essential knowledge from an experienced mentor to new assistants and apprentices might be lost and 'replaced' by tool-intensive training alone.

I hope this book can help preserve that vibrant, more complete way of learning.

– rdp

acknowledgements

Thank you Betsy and Christopher for your never-ending encouragement, beneficial criticisms, and an abundance of helpful ideas.

Andy and Ollie, I thank you for your patience, and companionship, at the computer.

Thank you Jack Haber. You took my job search telephone calls — from March 1963 through February 1964 — at Mecca Film Lab. You never, not once, sounded irritated by my imposing upon your busy schedule; nor were you ever exasperated by my continuing reminder that I had no film experience nor knowledge. You invited me to the Film Center Building, and introduced me to Bill Dorr at Liaison Films.

Thank you Bill for giving me "Three days to learn how to track read" for the animated *Tennessee Tuxedo* and *Underdog* shows. Somehow, though I was initially convinced that track reading was impossible to learn, I did. You let me assist the shows' editor Corky Smith.

Thank you Corky. You taught me to cement splice on a grand old foot pedal model, and to use the Upright Moviola — a noisy green hazard, until I mastered the thing. Later you called with a job offer at East-West Films. You introduced me to Armond Lebowitz.

Thank you Armond. You made me your assistant. You taught me how to simplify. I've yet to meet anyone who takes as much pleasure — or enjoys more intuitive talent — in being a film editor. Watching you work convinced me to stay in the editing room. The first film you 'turned over' to me was a documentary about the sounds and music of Polynesia, directed by Sid Shaw.

Thank you Sid. You were kindly tolerant as I made my way through your thousands of feet of material. You were a delight as a friend. One day you suggested that I would make a good teacher.

Thank you Mr. Silas Rhodes, Chairman of the School of Visual Arts, for the opportunity to teach at SVA; for your encouragement, and appreciation of my best efforts; and for your ongoing generosity to me, to colleagues, and to students.

Thank you Mr. David Rhodes, SVA President; Mr. Reeves Lehmann, Chairman of the Film, Video and Animation Department; Mr. Salvatore Petrosino, Director of

Operations; colleagues and staff at SVA. You have added heartwarming fulfillment to so many of my years.

Much of what I know results from the devoted learning of my students: They allowed me to 'touch' their work; they 'persuaded' me to be an everlasting pupil of film editing. I thank them.

Thank you Michael Wiese, Ken Lee, Paul Norlen, Gina Mansfield, Mark Pacella, Amy Taubin, and Barry Grimes. You have — no doubt about it — made my book (much) better.

preface

I've thought about writing a book ever since a student in my Advanced Editing class asked me if I'd read Ed Dmytryk's *On Film Editing*. I hadn't and said so. But I got the feeling that the student didn't believe me. "So much of what you're teaching is a lot like what Dmytryk writes about." I asked to borrow the book. I read it, and it became the first book about (or on) film editing that I required for my classes. It is still on my growing list of suggested readings.

It was comforting to find concurrence with many of my ideas on the subject. Good to see that I was not 'off-the-wall.' I understood the student's certainty that my syllabus was derived from Dmytryk's writings. Many of Dmytryk's proposals and approaches to "cutting" were comparable to my instruction. But, in truth, my syllabus was derived from many semesters struggling to learn what it was that I knew about film editing.

Teaching film editing is a few measures more complicated than being a film editor. Working does not necessitate comprehensive explanations or 'near scholarly opinions.' Teaching sometimes does.

The first thing I learned as a teacher was how much I trusted my instincts when I worked. I also learned how little I understood my instincts; and how my work experience had not only provided me additional know-how, but had also expanded the array and accessibility of my instincts. Like know-how, instincts are not stagnant. And finally, I learned how inconsequential my instincts and know-how would be if I couldn't find a way of communicating them to my students.

As it's turned out, I've been attempting to figure out instincts and know-how for decades. The abiding practice readies me as a teacher, and it has greatly improved my film editing.

From time to time the impulse to write a book would return. Two things would interrupt. Additional books about film editing, many very fine, would show up on bookshelves. And second, writing is an arduous undertaking. I found the first a good excuse not to write. What else need be uttered? The second was a powerful reason not to begin — especially after spending a good part of each week talking about film editing. Nevertheless, the impulse to write my book has come again.

Sam O'Steen said, "After you've (edited) for a long time, as I have, you've done all the cuts." The reader can be grateful that I delayed writing my book. With my many additional years — it's been more than fifteen since the student lent me the Dmytryk book — of working and teaching, I must surely know something about film editing; and I am now confident that my observations and comments are not presumptuous — my hair has thinned, and it is — well beyond 18% — gray.

I am optimistic that I can address some unexplored perspectives, and offer considerable practical guidance. The School of Visual Arts has graciously given me a sabbatical. I won't have to talk about film editing for a while. This will help make the writing chore more than manageable for me, and (I do very much hope) the reading beneficial for you.

I have chosen films for this book that I believe give clear and comprehensive illustration to the concepts and topics presented. Many of the examples come from the same films — at times from the same scenes. The fact is that all of the examples might well come from any single film — in large part, every film has every choice that can be illustrated. Several of my choices come from the work of my students.

I make no attempt to have you like or dislike any of the films that I've included; or to have you alter a previously held opinion about them. Long ago I learned that likes and dislikes develop from intricate personal associations and feelings; and that the pressures of popular culture — of which movies are a big part — pretty much forbid my considering, let alone giving, lessons in taste.

The maestro violinist Isaac Stern said it best, "You cannot force someone to think as you do, or to feel as you do, but you can teach them to think a little better, to think a little more, to listen more critically; to listen to what they're really doing, not what they think they're doing."

I am not offering film reviews, but reflections on editing choices, which exist in every film ever edited. There are editing judgments — one can argue forever whether judgment is subjective or objective — which most would agree do make a film better. I have participated in the editing of well over 5000 films, and been an eyewitness to more than several hundreds of thousands of revisions during the editing and re-editing process, and (nearly) all those observing the changes agreed that they made an auspicious difference. By no means am I taking credit for each and every improvement — spotting 'problems,' and suggesting solutions, are offered by a great many collaborators in the postproduction process. I am proposing that there are lots more objectively reliable choices than you might suppose. The requisite purpose of this book is to examine the possibilities, to illustrate their worth, and to prove that you can always think more critically.

Frequently it is the simplest — the tiniest — of touches that provide the greatest advantage. Yet, it is unexpectedly tricky to simplify. All great work is simultaneously complex — not complicated — and simple. Jazz bassist and composer Charlie Mingus pointed this out: "Making the simple complicated is commonplace; making the complicated simple, awesomely simple, that's creativity."

I believe it is possible to understand — as in "I see" — what is common, and constant, in all great work. Although it is never easy to achieve, it is imperative — I don't know that there's a choice — to make the attempt.

This book is not about theory. When I work I do what's practical; that's what I teach, and that's what I've written — what to look for; what to look out for; what works, and why. I have attempted to present an ordered assembly of principles, methods, strategies, examples, and distinctive techniques in the art of creative film editing. Truly creative editing is nonlinear in process; and frequently, so is creative learning. To sustain this idea within a linear book I have included HINTS to link topic to topic — back and forth; and TIPS to emphasize chapter topics, and provide highlights on work concepts.

I now approach forty years of work, and thirty years of teaching. I've done 'all the cuts!' Here is what I've learned about film editing from students, colleagues, teaching, and working. *The Eye is Quicker* is an ongoing chat, offering a collection of wherewithal, and handy know-how, from which to make yourself a better — maybe even a far better — film editor. I wish the reader enjoyment and discovery.

foreword

As a film critic, I know only too well how little recognition is given to editors. To my chagrin, I have often ignored the best of them in my reviews. In a film culture where directors rule (in theory if not always in practice) and stars are mass audience magnets, it can sometimes seem as if no one else's work counts in the making of a movie. Oh yeah, we sometimes praise the cinematography (the adjective "ravishing" is much in vogue) or we might quibble that a script is "incoherent," but editing — who knows what that entails. And yet, some of the reviews of which I'm most proud give credit to editors: to Dede Allen for making *Wonder Boys* swing; to Susan Littenberg for evoking, with one or two remarkable cuts, the desperate feeling of impossible love in the low-budget romantic comedy *Tadpole*; to Thelma Schoonmaker for her rapier cutting of the knife-throwing scene in *Gangs of New York*, a movie redeemed by her work and the acting of Daniel Day-Lewis.

Still, I was surprised that my immediate reaction to Richard Pepperman's *The Eye Is Quicker* was to want to believe in reincarnation so that I could come back as a film editor. Critics, as we all know, tend to be power-mad exhibitionists. Nothing could be more opposed to the temperament of the ideal editor, who must be self-effacing, collaboratively inclined, and an obsessive puzzle-solver in a situation where finding the solution may be the only reward. The better the editor, the more invisible her or his work will be and the more likely that the director will get all the kudos. But what could be more rewarding than the kind of immersion in editing that Pepperman, using his 40 years of experience as an editor and teacher of editing, vividly evokes. *The Eye Is Quicker* is a rare guidebook in that it is both practical and inspirational. It appeals to the head and the heart, and one of the first lessons Pepperman teaches is about the necessity of applying both to the task at hand.

As Martin Scorsese has often remarked, every time one makes a picture, one feels as if one has to learn to do it all over again from scratch. In that sense, Pepperman's ability to lay out basic strategies and techniques and to warn about possible pitfalls makes this book useful even to experienced editors. But unlike so many books about editing, which describe the relationship between an editor and the many famous directors he or she has worked with, this book is filled with examples of students editing their own material or material directed by classmates. It is, therefore, students of all ages that will find *The Eye Is Quicker* an invaluable guide each time they set out on the absorbing, tricky, and thrilling journey of editing a movie.

Amy Taubin

Amy Taubin is a contributing editor for *Film Comment* magazine and *Sight and Sound* magazine. Her book, *Taxi Driver*, was published in 2000 in the British Film Institute's Film Classics series.

ONE

the eye
is quicker

"In all films, good or bad, cinematic
poetry struggles to reveal itself."

— Luis Buñuel

I encourage students to develop their skill at storytelling: Structure, Inflection, and Pacing. At times, I'll ask a student to stop editing, and tell me their story in a crisp, direct, and focused way. Film editing is — in utility — about storytelling. It is a unifying blend of story, delivery — techniques in conveyance, manner, and tone. Film editing is rendering storytelling delivery in images: The story is introduced to the eye. Better yet, film editing is all about storyshowing.

Let me begin with a story that will help set in motion many practical ideas, and guidance for making a good film better.

When my evening classes are workshops, I teach until 10:00 p.m. I take a taxi from the School of Visual Arts to Pennsylvania Station for the train ride home to New Jersey. My wife was uneasy about my walk across 23rd Street and uptown to 31st Street at such a late hour. I insisted that it was safe, "There are lots of people on the streets of New York all night long." My wife persisted, "That's just it, they could be dangerous people. Promise you'll take a taxi." I promised.

After finishing my class, I'd walk from the editing room, down five flights of stairs, hand my roster to the security officer at the front desk, exchange a "Goodnight," and exit the building raising my hand to hail a cab. Remarkably, in strict synchronization, a taxi would roll across 23rd Street in precise timing to my arrival at curbside. When you work in film, such things occur — just like in the movies!

Then one night there was no taxi. I saw some with their 'Off-Duty' light illuminated. A few approached, but were occupied.

A hurried walk to Penn Station from SVA takes scarcely less than 20 minutes. My train is the scheduled 10:35. After several minutes I began walking west on 23rd Street. I looked back again and again, checking for a cab.

I walked all the way to 6th Avenue before coming to a red light. To continue to the station without having to stop, I turned right, and began walking uptown along the avenue. More than likely I was going to catch my train, but I was badly into promise breaking.

I was less apprehensive about an encounter with a mugger, than troubled by a threatening irony. Would my broken promise — and first late night walk to catch the train — lead to my murder?

At 26th Street the light was red to uptown traffic, so I crossed 6th Avenue and walked west on the north side of the street.

Suddenly, somewhere between 6th and 7th Avenues, I flinched! I heaved my shoulders upward, simultaneously dropping my body in a ducking action. In an instant my arms were defending my face and head. There was no attacker. The street was without a single (or dangerous) person. I was thankful.

As it turned out, my quick protective moves were in reaction to my hair wavering into the peripheral sight of my right eye. I had automatically reacted to safeguard my life. That no cognitive appraisal was required to 'duck and cover' got me thinking.

I was twelve years old when my father purchased our first television. He surprised the family with a 13-inch Motorola. As were all TVs then, it was a black-and-white set. I hadn't missed much during my years without a television. There were very few programs — I remember watching station patterns on a cousin's set; they held interminably, accompanied by a fixed tone. We also had an open invitation from upstairs neighbors — the first family in the building to own a television — to join them every Tuesday evening at eight to watch the *Texaco Star Theater*, with Milton Berle.

But soon after my twelfth birthday we had a television in the kitchen of our apartment.

On Sunday evenings, before having to turn in for the night to begin the next school week, I was permitted to watch the *Ed Sullivan Show*. Mr. Sullivan was a columnist with the *New York Daily News* and hosted his own variety program, which featured every known form of entertainment. I took special pleasure in the magicians. I was awed by their flamboyance, their mind-boggling illusions, and in the over-all anticipation of their acts.

A few of my uncles could do some amazing card tricks; could even 'pull' a quarter out of my ear. But magicians on the *Ed Sullivan Show* were world-class.

I entered Penn Station. I thought about the assertive power the eye holds among all the senses; and of all the expressions which 'give voice' to this fact — and then some: See if the soup's any good; see if it's cold outside; see what I mean? I recalled that in the earliest days of MTV I overheard two young boys talking about a new album release. One asked, "Have you *seen* the new Michael Jackson song?"

I boarded the 10:35 train. I was safe. I had protected myself from my longish hair — the only peril en route. But my memory had been jogged. I remembered the *Ed Sullivan Show*, and something my father told me.

One Sunday evening, while my family watched one of Ed's magicians, my father offered up the 'secret' of their incredible practiced craft. "The hand is quicker than the eye!" I have heard the assertion many times. It is not true. The eye is quicker! This fact is indispensable for film editors. It holds a very simple significance: Directly it means that the moment selected for the joining of images must be 'calculated' to the very speedy interpretive facility of our eyes — a specific **cut** can work well or poorly. It is equally fundamental to our ability to 'decode' collections of images: The eye is ever alert to 'take in' information, and swift to embrace intricate descriptions. The eye is quicker than you might envision to 'get the picture.'

mind watching
the cuts

*"Editing is the creative force of
filmic reality."*

— V. I. Pudovkin

Have you ever watched the eyes of passengers as a subway train enters a station? Their pupils switch briskly from left to right. The passengers are trying to read the posted street signs on the platform pillars.

Some half-dozen years before my family was able to watch television programs on our own set, my father would, on many a Sunday morning, take my younger sister, me, and a large bag of unshelled peanuts, on the subway. We traveled to Times Square to feed pigeons. We were on the train for some six or seven stops, and I would make the trip uptown an 'undercover' adventure — I would surreptitiously watch people's eyes. The repositioning of the pupils, in speed and range, is spectacular. Our eyes are as resolutely watchful when fixed on a movie screen. While they might not affect the same subway dance, we know they take great pleasure as images boogie, tap, and waltz.

There is delight to the eye as diverse compositions cut into sight. The appeal is so marvelous that the eye can easily be dazzled without regard to substance; in the same way sweets can seduce the tongue without regard to sustenance. Could this provoke a discussion about the integrity of Sugar Sweet Puff Cereal, and film editing?

At least three million years — I apologize, but I must speed through them and stay attentive to my point — of the human eye giving us an on-the-spot defensive reflex have predestined our survival; and the astonishing capacity of our eyes to absorb information — as well as gain pleasure — has predetermined the emergence and evolution of the visual arts.

Yet, with all the history — and my hasty prehistory — of the quick-eye's reflex, the asserted aim of the film editor is to craft the **invisible cut**. Is it possible for cuts to go undetected? In an effort to check my 'eye is quicker' brainchild, I tried a straightforward test.

I asked my students to watch a scene presented via a VCR and monitor, and to raise a hand whenever they became aware of a cut. I played the scene, and hands went-up. No student failed to spot each and every cut. Not a single cut went unobserved!

If CUTS are discernible — and with very few exceptions they are — what are film editors determined to achieve? How can the audience sit undistracted by the starkness of frequent cuts? Why do some cuts produce disconcerting obviousness? Or, quite simply, are there **good cuts** and **bad cuts**? If there are, what are their attributes?

Certain characteristics inescapably engage the eye. The principal eye-catcher is movement. Remember my longish hair?

Out of this knowledge about movement and the eye has come the timeless adage: Cut on Action. This is a simple practice to facilitate a safe cut — a cut that is more or less inconspicuous. Cutting on action doesn't promise an invisible cut, but at times it is one of the few exceptions illustrating the possibility of an (almost) undetectable cut. Continuous frames of film — at 24 frames per second — depict movement. Even in the finest focused shot, single frames of movement can reveal various degrees of blur. The more extreme the movement, the greater is the likelihood of blur in any single frame. If shots are joined at frames of extreme action — and greatest blur — the eye might fail to spot the cut; and sometimes no hand will go up — at least not so quickly.

You can see — but not so easily — an example of this 'blur effect' in the Cadets Exercise in the Courtyard scene, from *Colonel Redl*. During the push-ups drill [*Figure 2.1*] a cut is made after young Alfred Redl looks down — the top of his cap facing the camera. The incoming cut to young Kristof Kubinyi is instantly recognizable because Kristof is facing the camera.

Figure 2.1

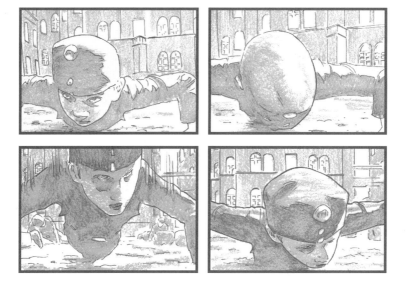

Later, during the squat-jumps drill, a cut is again made from young Alfred to young Kristof, but this time both boys are facing the camera, at a moment of excessive blur. [*Figure 2.2*] You may need to watch more than once to...

Figure 2.2

...catch sight of the cut

Very few cuts exhibit such characteristics. Most often the movement is modest, with only slight blur displayed. But the blur factor must be considered when a cut results in disconcerting obviousness. There are instances when a cut is disturbing because the movement (however slight), effects a trifling of blur in the Outgoing frame that exceeds (or is less than) the blur in the Incoming frame. The quick-eye will spot this hitch: a hesitating, or faltering of sorts. Ed Dmytryk refers to cuts that initiate such a sudden starkness as "mental hiccups!" The "mental hiccup" cut is conspicuous, and can be considered a 'bad cut.'

TIP: The 'imbalanced blur' bad cut can be made good by 'seeing' that there is a more, rather than a less, equal degree of blur on both sides of the cut. There are lots of times when an adjustment of a single frame will make all the difference.

The most common "mental hiccup" is triggered when a cut — made too soon after a movement begins — doesn't allow for an 'evolution' from the quick-eye's reflex to a mindful response. In other words, the eye responds to the movement with quick vigilance while the conscious brain wonders, "What was that?" If you say, "What was that?" as fast as you can, that's something akin to a "mental hiccup."

These bad cuts can be made good by either trimming the Outgoing cut of the motion that has grabbed the eye, or by adding 2-3 frames to the Outgoing (extending the movement), thus allowing a mindful response. The latter is very helpful when a swift movement grips the eye: a quick head turn, or a hand speed-ing upward. Extending the movement by 2-3 frames creates an **extended** action across the cut. Interestingly, this kind of cut can be obvious when viewed in slow motion or in reverse, revealing repetitiveness, or a near-doubling of the action; yet the extended cut works wonderfully well when viewed forward at normal (24 fps) speed.

For a great example of a Quick Head–Turn, and its extended cut in action, screen Jack Returns to "Grandfather" scene from *Little Big Man*.

After exchanging greetings, Jack learns that Grandfather has been wounded, and is blind. Jack is told that the "white man" is responsible; and he quickly turns his head to look for "Buffalo Walla Woman." Concentrate on Jack's face. The action of the head-turn begins with the camera facing Jack's front. The extended cut of the head-turn is completed with the camera at Jack's back — as he turns and faces the camera. [*Figure 2.3*]

Figure 2.3

See if you can spot the near doubling of the head-turn.

All cuts exist within the margin of two film frames: the Outgoing and the Incoming. A cut across action must take into account another equally decisive feature of the 'quick-eye' reflex: how does the eye 'read' the spatial illusion of the projected image. Film is a two-dimensional rendition of space, and if a Quick-Head-Turn is joined — on either side of the cut — with the head in precise pro-file, the cut can be perceived as 'paused.' This is especially true if the frame in profile contains too little blur. The profile calls attention — in the quick-eye — to the film's two-dimensional presentation. The profile is (often) 'read' as a still frame. This is true for all cuts across a continuing action: a spinning ballerina, with an Outgoing or Incoming cut at the moment her body is precisely aligned, in profile or straight ahead, or arms correspondingly matched — parallel to the background — eliminating the foreshortening that visually 'implies' three-dimensions, will likely be perceived as 'paused.' [*Figure 2.4*]

Figure 2.4

HINT: There'll be more about film's two-dimensional rendition of three-dimensional space.

The spinning ballerina presents a good lesson in **focal point**. The etymology of the word 'focus' is of special interest; and curiously, the definitions of the word 'interest' are immediately allied to those of 'focus': attention; notice; awareness. 'Focus' is of Latin derivation meaning 'hearth', as in fireplace — literally the French 'foyer.' Remember my mentioning that 'movement' is the principal eye-catcher? Movement, and whatever (else) catches the eye — even within a single film frame — is the focal point. Light catches the eye, and fire (or fireplace) attaches to the derivation of 'focus.'

TIP: A cut that captures too brief a shifting in light — a lamp coming on or going off — will conspicuously catch the eye; it might require an extended cut.

After movement comes people. Our eyes will take quick and immediate notice of people. The face takes preference. The eyes take greater preference. A blink of the eyes — there is movement — is of paramount preference, as would a change in facial expression(s): shifting eyes, mouth, or brow. If any of these facial expressions just barely begin, and a cut is made prior to a 'mindful response,' you'll end up with a "mental hiccup."

How does a face as focal point influence the example of the spinning ballerina? To our eyes a spinning ballerina is principally — or 'prima' — a spinning face. If a cut is made during her spin, with preference given to the position of her face — being certain that the cut 'conceals' the fact that the movie screen is flat, [*Figure 2.5*] and that there is an equal distribution of 'blur' — it will, in all likelihood, be successful even if the ballerina's arms or legs do not match across the cut, because the audience's eyes will be concentrated on the face.

Figure 2.5

Successfully spinning a 'mismatch'

TIP: In all cases, if you can find the focal point — where your eyes inevitably gaze — you can 'find' (or fix) a cut!

There are occasions when something weirdly jarring happens at a cut. This is more than likely a result of your quick-eye reflex doing its job. The eyes dart to a sector of the film frame when a movement alerts them more rapidly than the brain's cognitive appraisal can bear it in mind: "What was that?" Watch the cut again. Do you 'see' what your eyes saw?

TIP: Use your hands to cover all but the portion of the screen that you thought your eyes were watching. If the cut now seems to work, look again, this time full screen, and you're certain to find the movement your eyes spotted. It might be the boom microphone dipping into view at the frame's top; or an actor you 'thought' went unobserved, shifting his hand, or eyes. With some practice — that'll come with experience — you will develop the uncanny facility to have your brain 'watch and note' your eyes' automatic responses.

The truth is that cuts are no more invisible than the film image itself is invisible. Film is, in large part, given life by the indispensable cut; and the moment of the join can be apparent and trouble-free at the same time. In much the same way we can point to isolated words on a page, and separate sounds which make up words. But we are not truly reading unless the eye-brain disregards the parts for the whole. We are not wholly listening unless we draw together the words into sentences, into ideas and meaning.

Plainly put, the good film editor strives to join the many film fragments, so that the structure established might hold enchantment, with no attentive concern about a cut. If there is form and purpose the audience can be captivated by the experience. In all creative storytelling, whether film, theatre, or literature, the aim is the same: have the fragments fade, and what remains is the harmony of the whole.

Editing lends an important hand in the fragment-fading process of good film-making. It is the foundation of Dmytryk's depiction of editing as "the essence of motion pictures."

Students — and young filmmakers — are inclined to be absorbed with cut after solo cut. I would not expect the earliest spotlight on the editor's work to be any different. So yes, keep an eye on the cuts, but if you follow the suggestions in this chapter, you will see — as quick as your eye — that every single cut can be made inconspicuous.

HINT: I did not propose a dissolve as a 'fix.'

In time you'll find that 'winning cuts' are so simple to accomplish that their satisfying pleasure will be fleeting. You will come 'to see' that they are not the editor's definitive achievement. The triumph is to be found in the sensations and unity of the entire film.

editing with
two left feet

"I never cut for matches, I cut for impact."

— Sam O'Steen

The prominence of the cut, and the determined security to cut on action explain the inescapable lure to match action.

Let's remember the "Quick Head Turn," and the effective extended cut. Wanting to match this swift movement across a cut originates in a common and curious assumption: Editors strive to duplicate real life; consequently, time and movement across a cut should be a picture of authenticity. The student filmmaker takes a count of frames from the shots showing the head turn, and divides by two. If it takes six frames for a "Quick Head Turn," half of the movement, or three frames of action can be held to the Outgoing cut, and three frames of the completed action can begin the Incoming. This should deliver authenticity, and a 'good cut.' Most often it doesn't. Remember "mental hiccups"?

Let's not consider a "Quick Head Turn" that takes five frames — I don't do fractions. First of all, film is not reality. It is 'life' presented in a staccato start/stop cinematographic pulse. Several set-ups (or angles) are filmed. The actions (and dialogue) are repeated in each set-up. The recurring actions are neither precise in time nor gesture. If you take into account the assortment of angles, camera distances, and lens choices on an action, you'll see that actions can be positioned in a wide range of frame sectors, and in an array of sizes.

TIP & HINT: Don't disregard the effects of film's two-dimensional presentation.

If your singular concern is to cut on action, you might be 'closing your eyes' to the necessities of the scene. Is the scene about a "Quick Head Turn"?

HINT: What about the comprehensive plan of the scene, sequence, or the entirety of the film?

TIP: Think big — from extensive to vast. It is best not to begin with a concentration on cuts. You can double — and then some — the actions across cuts. This will allow you a diversity of opportunities (later) when the needs of the scene are unmistakable.

You might discover that you don't have to cut on action at all. You can let the "Quick Head Turn," (or any action) be completed in an ongoing shot. I've heard that John Huston would admonish editors who took time 'matching' actions — especially actions of someone sitting or standing — across a cut. He'd point out, "This scene is not about sitting or standing!"

All right! You are — regardless of John Huston — determined to cut across the "Quick Head Turn." If you try to match the action, after dividing the frame count by two, and halving the action on either side, you will, in all probability, be facing a "mental hiccup," because — remember — the quicker the action the more its Outgoing movement is needed before the cut. This 'mismatch' will likely appear as a 'match.' But! Frequently something else will 'trouble' your eye. Depending upon the shifting position within the frame, or the variability in scale, the cut may 'insist' upon a further extending, or sometimes a **compressing** of the action.

A woman is sitting on a park bench. After some seconds she stands. Here is a fine instance to identify the influence of film frame location on action and cuts. By the way, this is an example from a student's film. There are two compositions (set-ups) depicting the action. [*Figure 3.1*]

Figure 3.1

A Medium Shot preceded a Long Shot

To cut during the standing action, so that it 'matches' across the cut, the student figured: If I calculate the distance from the bench to the woman's bottom I can match precisely across the cut. How far is the woman's bottom from the bench in the Outgoing, and therefore, where must the bottom be in the Incoming in order for there to be accuracy of action? The student did this calculation — quite precisely — and made the cut. He was baffled when it didn't work.

The student's cut didn't work because our eyes watch the woman's face, not her bottom. When the woman starts to stand, the key to the cut is the reference of her face — her eyes — within the film frame.

HINT: A person on screen will be the focal point — the eyes' focus. A face takes preference. The eyes take greater preference. If you 'find' the focal point you'll 'find the cut.'

We are watching the woman's face throughout her upward movement. The film frame has a Top and Bottom. This Bottom and (in this example) the Top are most important. The first shot is a Medium Shot. In this composing the woman is already near, or at, the frame's Top; when the woman stands, her face (nearly) disappears in the Outgoing frame. The student's initial cut, however accurate the position of the woman's bottom, had the Incoming Long Shot portraying the woman's face well below the Top of the frame. [*Figure 3.2*] The Incoming shot 'persuaded' our eyes that the woman's face had moved downward — because it did — within the scope of the frame.

Figure 3.2

For an instant the woman appears to re-sit

TIP: It is best to avoid having the eyes (we are watching) clear the frame — at least not both. If the Outgoing frame of the woman standing doesn't retain her eyes, a kind of "mental hiccup" occurs: an established focal point vanishes across the cut.

Before solving the 'Bottom and Bench' editing puzzle, let me give a couple of examples of **maintaining the focal point** across a cut: The Butcher Changes a Light Bulb scene, from an SVA thesis film, *Alicia Was Fainting*. The butcher, atop a ladder, replaces a bulb in the freezer compartment's light fixture. He tosses the burned-out bulb to Alicia — his apprentice — who is standing at the ladder's base. A cut was made across the action of the falling bulb. [*Figure 3.3*] It did not matter where, in real-life time or space, the bulb should be, but only that it is discernible across the cut, and in relative proximity within the scope of the Outgoing and Incoming frames.

Figure 3.3

No matter how brief the time on screen, the eye 'catches' the bulb.

Alicia Was Fainting
Director/Editor Núria Olivé-Bellés

The next example involves the magical disappearance of the protagonist. Maya Arrives at the Lakeside Cottage scene from the thesis film, *Nowhere, Now Here*. A Long Shot from inside the automobile that has brought Maya, lets us see the cottage, and the attorney who has been awaiting her arrival. Maya and her driver exit the auto — the camera is behind them — and both walk toward the attorney. Initially, a cut was made — after several **beats** — to a Medium Long Shot from behind the attorney. [*Figure 3.4*] The initial consideration in selecting a cut point was the 'real-life' position of the three characters in the setting.

Figure 3.4

Something peculiar happened. Maya vanished!

Nowhere, Now Here
Director, Sako Pajari; Editor, Zohra Zaka

It was essential to lose a few frames on the Incoming shot so as to reveal — at least a bit of — Maya's face, coming from behind the attorney, and have the three characters 'spotted' immediately — especially Maya, the focal point. [*Figure 3.5*] This cut worked.

Figure 3.5

We can continue to see our protagonist across the cut

The solution to the 'Bottom and Bench' puzzle was simple: Since the scope of the frame, its Top and Bottom; its Left and Right, presents a better bearing for cuts across action than does real life, we intentionally 'mismatched' the (woman's) bottom's distance from the bench with an adjustment which made the cut at an earlier moment in the initial action, so that the woman's face was not as close to the frame's Top on the Outgoing — and her eyes never exited the frame. We made the cut later in the action of the Incoming shot, which brought the woman's face closer to the frame's Top at the cut point. [*Figure 3.6*] It is not required to tally the exact distance to the frame's Top.

Figure 3.6

There is some leeway: a sort of grace space.

There are three divergent, yet interrelated, models that address the proposition, **forget matching action**. First, there are some things that cannot be expected to match, no matter how precise the production. Second, there are some things the director will intentionally not want to produce as a match. And third, finding the requirements of a scene frequently requires the editor to disregard matching altogether, integrating action and dialogue within daring mismatches that are 'unseen' by the audience, and most crucial, capture the absorbing essentials of the scene.

Let me suggest that you screen *Little Big Man* for the first two models:
1. Jack and Mrs. Pendrake in the Brothel scene. Keep your eyes on the beaded curtain during the seduction. [*Figure 3.7*] It moves at varying rates — at times nearly stopping — only to be followed by a cut showing it moving swiftly.

Figure 3.7

Continuous bead sounds, and other–than the curtain–focal points 'hide' the mismatches

2. Jack Returns to "Grandfather" scene. Jack leans closer to Grandfather's face upon learning he's blind. Yet, on the following cut (from) behind Jack, his position has not changed. [*Figure 3.8*] If the director had required Dustin Hoffman (Jack) to lean closer to Chief George (Grandfather), so as to match the reverse camera set-up, Dustin Hoffman would have blocked Chief George's face — rendering the shot useless.

Figure 3.8

The 'mismatch' makes the shot useable

Remember the "Quick Head-Turn" in the same scene? [*Figure 3.9*] Watch Chief George across that cut. Look at the Chief's right arm — yet another mismatch — but your eyes favor the movement of the head-turn. Here is a good reason to have cut on action.

Figure 3.9

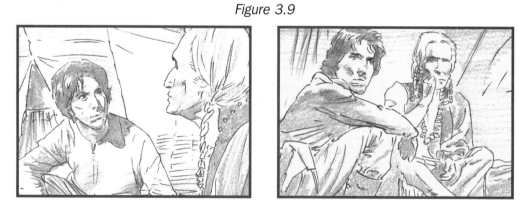

Movement is eye-catcher is focal point

Screen *The French Connection* for an exquisite example of the last model:
3. 'Popeye' Doyle and Russo Rough Up a Suspect scene. Undercover cop Doyle
wears a Santa suit; Russo is disguised as a hot dog vendor. Keep your eye on
Russo as he moves about the alleyway, [*Figure 3.10*] disappearing from the frame
in one shot, only to reappear in the next.

Figure 3.10

Isn't this fantastic?

The vital stratagem used in the success of the Doyle and Russo scene is the
meticulous treatment of the Suspect's face — especially his eyes: The
Suspect's eyes 'respond' to Doyle and Russo's Dialogue. The eyes quickly direct
the audience's 'focus,' and acceptance — motivating the cuts — of an otherwise
non-existent continuity.

Model #3 can also be viewed in Jack Returns to "Grandfather" scene. Watch Chief
George through all the cuts: His actions (hands up; hands down; hands moving;
hands still) and dialogue synchronization (lips moving in speech, sometimes

chewing; sometimes not) nearly never match. [*Figure 3.11*] This example is the more common form of action/synchronized sound 'mismatches,' which doesn't preclude successful editing.

Figure 3.11

A creative necessity

HINT: More to come on the creatively expansive 'nature' of synchronized sound.

For a perfect illustration of 'mismatching' brilliance, boldness, and the editor's ability to 'find' a moment's emotional essence, screen Frank and Family 'Celebrate' His Graduation from the Police Academy scene, from *Serpico*. After the ceremony, the family gathers outside the Police Academy. When they see Frank, [*Figure 3.12*] one of his brothers-in-law shouts, "Frankieeeee!" The brother-in-law's different arm gesture — along with "ieee!" — crosses the cut. No match at all, but undoubtedly the spirit of a celebratory gathering.

Figure 3.12

"Cut for proper values rather than for proper matches."

— Ed Dmytryk

Which foot follows the left when a person walks? The right foot is a good bet in real life, but in film the question is not answerable — until a cut is joined. Determinations in movement; frame sector; focal point; and the values of the scene, can guide the film editor to decide on a cut — a very fine cut — describing a walker with rhythmic charm, stepping left, right, left, left!

HINT: More later about rhythm; with perhaps a bit of charm.

Good editors are not to be discovered among those who have a shrewdness for determining — within centimeters — the incremental movements of bottoms, bulbs, and turning heads. If meticulous exactness were required, film editing would not be possible; and if editing were impossible, making movies would be out of the question.

small time operators

"*The development of film technique has been primarily the development of editing.*"

— Ernest Lindgren

Now that we've put Matching Action 'behind' us — so to speak — let's look at several approaches to purposeful mismatching. Interestingly, there are more than a few regularly employed which are so wholly accepted that you might wonder why anyone ever thinks matching action matters a whit.

First, let's get video editing clichés out of the way: the doubling, tripling, quadrupling — or even the quintupling — of an identical shot, and the 'every other cut goes to black' structure, which allows Outgoing and Incoming cuts of any kind to go anywhere, at anytime. These maneuvers are among the instigators that link sugary sweet cereal and film editing. Although deliberate, they are not so much 'purposeful' as 'purposeless' affect.

The approaches that I'm talking about are genuine and effective techniques to handle brief — to very brief — references in time. They fall into two categories: **perceptible** and **imperceptible structures**.

These structures are frequently utilized, often integrated, and offer creative promise to 'mismatched' cuts.

Perceptible Structure:
>   1. Jump Cut(s)
>   2. Overlapping Action(s)

Imperceptible Structure:
>   1. Jump Cut
>   2. Protracted Action(s).

The classic Jump Cut occurs when one or several frame(s) are deleted from an otherwise continuous camera run or shot. It is often employed in a series. Screen Frank Galvin Trashes His Office scene from *The Verdict*. Drunk, publicly embarrassed, in despair, and angry, Galvin 'destroys' his law office. The throwing and breaking of items is displayed with perceptible structured cuts: Jumps in Actions — the 'gaps' in time — are obvious. [*Figure 4.1*] What is skillfully effective is the asymmetrical approach to the Jump Cuts: They are integrated with a more traditional cut.

Figure 4.1

A good example of cutting for value and impact — not matches

HINT: Keep Asymmetrical in mind!

Sergei Eisenstein frequently made use of the other model of perceptible structures: Overlapping Actions. For a couple of examples of Eisenstein's handiwork screen The Battle on Ice scene, from *Alexander Nevsky*, and The Livestock Slaughter scene, from *Strike*.

Alexander Nevsky: As the mounted German Knights are about to clash with the Russian peasant army, Eisenstein uses multiple cuts of the Russians' lowering wooden staffs, used as spikes against the mounted knights. The lowering, and aiming action, is repeated, but from numerous perspectives — showing different segments of the Russian defensive line. It is clear by way of the repetitiveness, that the action — and time — is being overlapped. [*Figure 4.2*] The effect is to have the audience hold its breath — or gulp forcefully — in expectation of the powerful collision of armies.

Figure 4.2

Strike: Three shots capture a repeated action at a slaughterhouse. [*Figure 4.3*] A butcher mightily jabs a sharp instrument to the head of a steer, dropping it to the ground in preparation for bleeding and butchering the animal.

Figure 4.3

Perceptible structures are especially common in Eisenstein's films. Ed Dmytryk, in *On Film Editing*, deftly describes a scene from *The Old and the New*, in which a Soviet government instructor lifts a cloth — in multiple overlapping action shots — revealing a mechanical cream separator in front of an audience of peasant farmers, "with the flourish of a magician."

Jump Cuts are, by their very definition, expected to be perceptible; but Jump Cuts can be utilized in the second model: imperceptible structures.

There are times when too many beats — too much time — elapse between preferred actions in a continuous camera run.

HINT: I've mentioned beats here, and earlier. Lots more ahead.

The editor wants both (or all) of the actions; doesn't want to 'play' all the time between actions; and doesn't want to use any other camera set-up depicting the actions. Eliminating frames following the end of one preferred action so that the other occurs more quickly — at your command — does not have to result in a perceptible structure Jump Cut.

A student film 'showed' a story of a young man who lived alone in a trailer, and worked each day in janitorial services at a nursing home. In Jack Mops the Hallway scene, from *Jack Murphy*, we follow Jack and his on-wheels mopping bucket down the hall. The camera 'leaves' Jack moving into a Close-Up on a door. Long after — a whole lot of beats — Jack and his mopping bucket have exited frame right, Jack re-enters, opens the door, and enters the room. Whatever precision in timing between actions might have been computed in production, in postproduction it was clear that a lot less time was needed between Jack's exiting frame right and his re-entrance.

In such cases, it is often assumed that the surest cut — one that will possess an imperceptible structure — should be made somewhere in the 'empty hallway' footage. In other words, let Jack leave the frame, and at some point in the 'stillness' of the empty hall make the first cut. Then, at some point in another 'still' frame, prior to Jack's return, make the second cut, and everything in-between gets deleted. This seldom works to perfection. Even with a locked down camera holding a rigid position, there is 'life' to a film frame. The 'life' can be the activity of the light-sensitive particles — the 'dancing' grain — that make up the emulsion onto which the photographic image is instilled — but not 'still' enough. The eye might spot the 'abrupt' altering within the visible grain. This is similar to making a cut in the ambient sound of a 'quiet' empty hall. You'd be surprised how obvious — to the ear — is the altered sound wave patterns of 'silence.'

Quite often a Jump Cut calls attention to itself — when you don't want it to — because a little something catches your eye: an ever-so-slight shifting of an object, or a break in patterns of light.

TIP: The best approach, in this imperceptible structure model of a Jump Cut, is to make a cut that corresponds to the instant — your choice of a frame within the shot of the 'empty hall' — that you 'feel' Jack should re-enter. Then, find the very first frame showing Jack re-entering — it might be his shadow that precedes him — and cut. Join that frame to the 'corresponds to the instant' frame of your initial cut. [*Figure 4.4*] This solution takes advantage of the quick-eye reflex, which will dart to the 'new' — and in movement — addition to the 'empty hall': Jack (or his shadow) re-entering screen Right.

Figure 4.4

The proof is in the timing

Jack Murphy
Director, Shawn Hicks; Editor, Chris Guidi

TIP: When, as in the *Jack Murphy* scene, the camera is in movement, the editor must find the moment (frame) when the camera comes to rest; or the cut will 'jump.' A piece of masking tape placed on the screen, aligned to a precise horizontal or vertical edge — in this case it was the doorjamb — will reveal if there is any more of the camera move.

Ideal use of the Protracted Action(s) model of imperceptible structure can be viewed in *Breaker Morant*, the Opening of the Court Martial scene. The British Army court martial officers, military attorneys, and the three Australian soldiers facing trial remove their hats and helmets. [*Figure 4.5*] In 'real life' the action(s) would occur simultaneously. In this film moment a mini-essay on the removal of military headwear is created.

Figure 4.5

Seeing the simultaneous one by one

There are cuts which utilize a Jump Cut approach without the Classic Jump. Basil Pascali Spies on Mr. Bowles scene, from *Pascali's Island*. Pascali 'breaks into' Bowles' hotel room, and searches his belongings. He finds a cane; the handle lifts out to reveal a sword. Pascali slides the sword back into the cane, and with hardly a beat, a cut 'shifts' Pascali to the far side of the room. He is opening a bureau drawer. [*Figure 4.6*] The 'sliding' sound of the sword returned to its cane, and the 'sliding' sound of the bureau drawer's opening make the cut doubly effective.

Figure 4.6

A little less perceptible than a Classic Jump Cut

HINT: The Jump-like-cut works here because care was taken to have a clear and full gesture to the Outgoing frame, and an immediate focal point at the Incoming frame — the opening the bureau drawer. This is crucial to avoid a "mental hiccup."

TIP: All models discussed in this chapter can be substituted for each other with as small an adjustment as a frame or two, which influences the audience's perception. Where, when, and how the editor begins or ends a selected shot, or shots, can change a perceptible structure to an imperceptible one. Each model can be defined by whether the audience's emotional involvement occurs in an instant: perceptible structure; or is unbroken: imperceptible structure.

it beats ticks and tocks

"Time is nature's way of keeping
everything from happening at once."

— Anonymous

Walter Murch, in his superb book, In The Blink Of An Eye: A Perspective On Film Editing, provides a credible analogy of the film editor's work in the era before digital technology. The physically lively labor of that era — it hasn't completely vanished; there are directors and editors still working the old-fashioned way — led Murch to see the editor as sculptor. Murch describes editing on an (Upright) Moviola as 'sculpting in clay' — an adding (pasting/patching) of selected takes to build up to the film's form; and editing on a (Flatbed) Steenbeck [*Figure 5.1*] as 'sculpting in marble' — a cutting down (chiseling) from large reels of uncut dailies to 'bring out' the film.

Figure 5.1

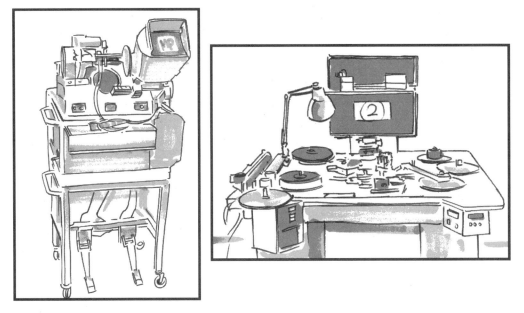

Moviola™   **Steenbeck™**

Director Andrei Tarkovsky broadens the 'editor as sculptor' analogy to include the entire realm of filmmaking in his memoir, *Sculpting in Time*. Tarkovsky's title expresses an abstract analogy — which offers a less tangible perspective than Murch — that helps me appreciate a vital correlation between cinema and humdrum perceptions of reality.

This chapter is not about mechanical, electronic, or digital editing tools. I'm writing to describe another useful device for the film editor; I guess in that way it can be considered a 'tool.' Not as in 'gizmo' or 'gadget,' but as a 'method' in work strategy reflections. It brings the physical analogy of Murch's 'editor as sculptor' to the 'conceptual atmosphere' of Tarkovsky's title.

This 'method' is reminiscent of the 'ticks and tocks' of a timepiece — editors are sculptors who bend, mold, and breach time — in semblance, not in exactness. Since, as we've already seen, or thought we were seeing, real-life 'matching action' has nothing to do with editing success, and in many ways is adverse to the best interests of a scene, so too the editor's 'timepiece' is neither accurate to the atomic clock or the heavens — and that's a very good thing. Film editing's 'timepiece-like-device' is not in 'ticks and tocks'; it's in beats.

You've likely seen the term in a screenplay; it (usually) directs the reader — or actor — to pause.

Sometimes the screenwriter might direct 'a couple of beats.' It may seem reasonable to assume that beats are, more or less, $1/2$ to one second in time. They can be, but with good old 'filmic reality' they are — to put it precisely — inexact.

Legend has it — I've been assured by actor friends it's accurate — that the use of the term beat is derived from a mishearing of Konstantin Stanislavsky's reference to an actor's 'bit.' Stanislavsky — the great acting theorist and teacher — was giving work technique tips with a view that suggested a 'breakdown' of a scene into tiny moments: bits. His Russian accent was 'translated' into beats. Beats or bits of moments might be an entrance or exit; movement on stage; engagement with objects or other actors; or segments — small(er) bits — of dialogue. It can be a helpful device, especially if several actors are 'working' with this reference. It allows for comprehensible discussions; and assessments can be (more) easily understood; and if needed, adjustments can be made to the subtlest or most elaborate workings of a scene.

A moment to moment to moment breakdown of a scene is an excellent 'tool' for the film editor; and I think it helpful to discuss early, so that any references to beats in later chapters, covering diverse concepts and examples, will be unmistakable; and will afford me a tidy way of describing, and elaborating on, particular topics.

HINT & TIP: Every moment can be identified, and beneficially estimated in beats: actions in time, and the 'time' in-between; lines of dialogue, and their emotional and/or subject matter variants. Beats can pinpoint trouble, and provide guidance for solutions.

It is not unusual for an editor (or director) to sense a 'rhythmic problem.' This means that a 'feeling' has been stirred that a pause, or a 'holding' (on a shot) of some additional 'time' is required; or that the opposite is needed — an existing beat, or two, shouldn't.

HINT: Later, how beats lead to **rhythms**, and their influence on the editor's choices and decisions.

Here are some examples of First-Rate and Faulty beats:

Hostages and Robbers Drive to Kennedy Airport scene(s), from *Dog Day Afternoon*. In a High Angle Shot, a white bus — holding the robbers and hostages — accompanied by police cars, drives toward the camera. The vehicles move from screen left to screen right, eventually moving off into the distance of the top of the screen. A cut takes us to a higher angle — aerial shot — as the caravan moves along an expressway. The vehicles are now moving screen right to screen left; and after a brief few beats — don't think about counting seconds so much as 'feeling that beat' — an overhead highway sign indicates the exit for Kennedy Airport. [*Figure 5.2*] The beats — without benefit of a stopwatch — before the overhead highway sign appears make it possible for an eye/emotion association to accept the journey from Brooklyn to the airport as 'conceivable' in time.

Figure 5.2

The edited beats create an Emotional Duration that 'feels' just right!

TIP: When editing, you can 'find' your choice beats backwards. The Kennedy Airport highway sign can be positioned on your screen first; then run the shot in reverse — back to the frame you 'feel' best furnishes the needed Incoming beats.

Realize that the selected beats of the Incoming aerial shot had to be unified with the Outgoing beats on the street in Brooklyn. For the Incoming beat to work, the Outgoing must work with it!

Here's an example of a Faulty 'One-Sided' beat:

John Proctor and the Arrival and Greeting of Reverend Hale scenes, from *The Crucible*. John is about to mount his horse when he hears a gathering crowd. He looks to screen right. In a Point Of View (POV) shot we see a crowd, and horse-drawn carriage. There is a cut back to John — a reaction beat which follows the POV shot. This shot holds on John as he begins to move to screen right: an ever-so-slight beat of John walking — although not exiting the frame — to greet the arriving Reverend.

The next cut brings us an Extreme Close-Up (ECU) of a stack of three books (perhaps Bibles and church law documents) on the carriage. Another (but very) brief beat holds this image. Hands enter the frame to take the books, and a cut takes us into a Medium Shot (MS) [*Figure 5.3*] as John arrives to greet Reverend Hale.

Figure 5.3

A quirk in Time? or is it Space?

The earlier POV shot of the crowd situated John a fair distance from the arriving Reverend. When the Medium Shot shows John almost to the carriage we are discordantly jolted. What has gone wrong, and why? Is it the beginning of John's walk; or his arrival; or the distance, or the books? Or is it a faulty selection, and integration of beats, that present a puzzling Emotional Duration?

HINT: A vital difference between theatre and cinema is the editing techniques that integrate beats.

Whenever 'real-life' time (or space) is a primary editing pursuit you will be risking far more (serious) audience confusion than if — through beats — you establish a sense — or texture — of the needed (psychological) time.

HINT & TIP: Don't only 'forget about matching action,' forget precise and realistic matching of anything! What is astonishingly elastic about 'film time' is that the most minor modification in beats can make all the difference.

The Extreme Close-Up of the Reverend's books needs to hold additional beats; or the Medium Shot of John's arrival needs additional beats before we spot him coming through the crowd; or eliminate the John-begins-to-walk beat. If the reaction back to John ended without any visual reference to his leaving that location, every other beat (with minor adjustment) would succeed. There would be no 'walking time' and therefore no reference to 'real time.'

There are other choices — there always are: Eliminate the reaction cut back to John — in other words, stay with the crowd and carriage from the Long Shot to the Extreme Close-Up of the books. Let the audience see the crowd in Long Shot before John looks to screen right — which indicates that he sees the crowd. Back up several beats to Abigail's last angry remarks to John, and let the crowd in sound and/or image 'motivate' her hurrying away before John looks to screen Right. [*Figure 5.4*] This last approach would integrate — something a HINT points out about theatre and cinema — a late beat of the John and Abigail Seduction scene (which is the preceding scene) with the John Sees the Arrival of Hale beat and the John Goes to Hale (an ironic pun) beat.

Figure 5.4

I imagine you're seeing the value of beats.

A second example of first-rate beats:

Rosemary Returns from the Cemetery scene, from *Rosemary's Baby*, skillfully demonstrates how beats offer a flexible and abstract treatment of film's Space/Time. Rosemary has no sooner arrived home than her doorbell rings. She looks toward the hallway, which leads to the apartment door. There is a slight 'hesitating' beat, and an even slighter, Rosemary 'rocks-back' beat — a 'feel' that Rosemary is about to walk forward. A cut now reveals a Close-Up of the apartment door — in a beat, no longer than the 'stack of books before the hands enter' beat, from *The Crucible* — as Rosemary is about to enter the frame, and open it. [*Figure 5.5*] It works. It's effective, and efficiently smart.

Figure 5.5

Elegant in its simplicity

Beats must be considered when joining one scene to another — creating a sequence:

Basil Pascali and the Arrival of Mr. Bowles scene precedes — by two scenes — the Pascali Arrives at the Hotel scene, from *Pascali's Island*. A very bright day, a crowd is gathered at the village dock for the arrival of a boat. Pascali is in the crowd. He observes one of the passengers — a tall man in a white suit. The man comes ashore, under Pascali's scrutiny.

The Hotel scene is at night. While possible to go directly to it — there is a Fade Out from the sunny dockside — several beats are included which dispense essential duration; provide a tangible atmosphere to the story and place; and most essential of all, carry the changes in dramatic inflection, faultlessly averting a hurried, sketchy feeling. [*Figure 5.6*]

HINT & TIP: A satisfying arrangement has to be discovered that eliminates superfluous beats, without leaving only a 'lifeless' (visual) synopsis.

Figure 5.6

Beats representing scene-to-scene 'delivery'

The first beat — which takes us into the night — is a single shot (a scene of several beats) looking upward to a nearly silhouetted minaret. A cut to another (night) scene shows soldiers, and their prisoner, marching along a street; followed by Pascali. He passes a group kneeling in prayer. A dissolve brings us to the Hotel scene. Pascali approaches a stairway which leads up to the hotel's entranceway.

HINT: Why the choice of a dissolve here — or any optical effect anywhere? What do optical effects do to beats?

Frank Galvin Meets the Sister scene(s), from *The Verdict*. In a Long Shot, Attorney Galvin returns to his office; he is 'late' for the appointment. The sister of his client has been waiting for him in the hallway. Galvin unlocks the door, and they enter the office. A very short beat follows the closing office door, ending the Hallway scene. A cut to a Medium Close Up of Galvin — his overcoat now off —

begins the Office scene. [*Figure 5.7*] A beat, which includes an inhale, leads to the first dialogue of the scene.

Figure 5.7

No superfluous beats, and dramatic breadth protected

TIP: *The Verdict* presents an example of organizing beats across 'Continuous Scenes' — INTERIOR HALLWAY to INTERIOR LAW OFFICE — that provide a successful departure from the usual technique of attempting to maintain 'real time' by following people from room to room, or from outside to inside.

Beats must be considered when joining sequence to sequence:

The Old Clown and Parrot scene, from *Burnt by the Sun*. [*Figure 5.8*] This scene is in response to a required beat, to 'deliver' an inflection change between Nadya Examines the Black Sedan scene, through Nadya and Colonel Kotov Play Games scene, which make up one sequence, [*Figure 5.9*] and the 'Family' Gathers Outside the Gate scene through the Shooting the Truck Driver scene, which make up the next sequence. [*Figure 5.10*]

Figure 5.8

A game of 'tease' with the parrot...

Figure 5.9

...joins 'games' from the end of the previous sequence to...

Figure 5.10

…an 'entertaining' send-off, which begins the next.

Last, an examination of superfluous — or overly extended — beats.

John Proctor Greets Reverend Hale scene, from *The Crucible*. John arrives at Reverend Hale's carriage. He takes a stack of books. Hale collects an additional stack.

JOHN PROCTOR
(taking note of the books' weight)
Heavy books!

REVEREND HALE
They must be; they're weighted with authority.

Reverend Hale smiles upon completion of his words. He then adds an additional beat — perhaps even two — of an overly satisfied smile, and cock of his head. [*Figure 5.11*]

Figure 5.11

A smile...and then some...and then some

JOHN PROCTOR
(reaching out his hand)
I'm John Proctor, Mr. Hale.

There is an obvious inflection change — beat change — from Hale's words to Proctor's greeting. That is, a 'pause' (beat) does seem necessary between Reverend Hale's response to "Heavy books" and John's reaching out to introduce himself. [*Figure 5.12*]

Figure 5.12

Beats, separated and extended, transform the subtext

The need for a beat — or two — could have been handled by integrating the "Weighted With Authority" beat with the "I'm John Proctor" beat: cut to John early in Hale's response; perhaps then cut back to Hale — or not — making use of overlapping dialogue. Hear John, but 'see' Reverend Hale; or hear Reverend Hale, but 'see' John.

As it stands, 'hanging' on Hale's smiling face for far too many beats — so as to carry us to the "I'm John Proctor" beat — the scheme in construction is palpable; and worse, the emotional subtext makes it 'appear' as if the Good Reverend is trying to seduce Proctor.

HINT: An understanding of how beat and rhythms motivate and establish **subtext** is fundamental to the editor's 'search' for actor performance.

TIP: It is helpful to give title designations to a film's scenes, the way I've done by 'labeling' my examples. Scenes will always have a number, but seldom is there an emotional — or content — imprint to material that is called, say, SCENE 42.

Descriptive designations will facilitate quick recall; and designating beats — that make up a scene — is exactly what this chapter is about! Having a 'tool' to help 'monitor' the 'sculpting in time,' will efficiently advance the editing. It will make it easier to 'work smart': Continually, and efficiently, remain focused and refine.

HINT & TIP: Early efforts in the postproduction process should be about assembling selected material in large strokes. It might better be expressed as putting-up 'spare time.'

juxt
about
right

"There is no art in confusion."

— Isaac Bashevis Singer

"On a blistering Brooklyn afternoon, two optimistic losers set out to rob a bank." This is the version of events on the back of the current VHS box for *Dog Day Afternoon*. When I saw the film at its release in the mid-1970s, it seemed to me that the time of day was not afternoon. I 'felt' that the opening montage 'illustrated' morning. Several friends reminded me of the film's title; they also pointed out that the opening montage included a shot of a clock — on a cigarette billboard — reading 2:57. How could I, the only one (of my friends) working in film, and a teacher of editing, have gotten it wrong?

When *Dog Day Afternoon* was first introduced for home video sale, I eagerly bought a VHS copy. I wanted to own one of the great American films. On the back of that VHS box it read: "On August 22, 1972, in the early morning heat of a scorching New York midsummer day, gunmen enter a local bank." The writer of this original text had to have seen the film. There is no way to get it wrong if your 'information' comes from the film's title.

Why had — at least — two people made the same mistake?

Sergei Eisenstein proposed that storytelling in cinema is at its best when constructed in an assembly of **juxtaposed images**. In *On Directing Film*, David Mamet 'confesses' that the juxtaposition of images is "the first thing I know about film directing, virtually the only thing I know about film directing." You can see from his 'admission' that Mamet's knowledge of film directing is exactly what is required for film editing. In *On Film Editing*, Ed Dmytryk (nearly) pleads for filmmakers to return to this simple notion of montage: It is the absolute essence of cinematic art.

An indiscriminate juxtaposition of images may not cause a "mental hiccup," but it is as disruptive — and confusing.

Dog Day's opening includes some 28 shots around New York City. They are meant — I'm guessing — to 'take the audience' from morning into afternoon. The shots are without order — they are uncommonly haphazard; and all too often, the collection of images re-depicts morning. The montage renders a hot summer day so effectively that I discounted the accuracy of the clock. I 'felt' that, because of the heat, the clock had malfunctioned — the 2:57 pops-off prior to the next cut. [*Figure 6.1*] It might have helped — but only a bit — to have held the clock till the time changed to 2:58!

Figure 6.1

I thought the 'malfunctioning' clock had died in the summer's heat!

The juxtaposition makes no allowance for the 'meaning' of particular images: What time of day comes to mind when you see a shopkeeper washing down the street; garbage trucks making pick-ups; or a traffic jam with vehicles approaching the camera? [*Figure 6.2*] Isn't the traffic approaching the city? Doesn't this signal morning rush hour?

Figure 6.2

'Morning' images are scattered throughout

It is a simple thing to juxtapose images — to put side by side. It's not easy to do it well. It is especially difficult to make (right) choices when the material is silent — without dialogue — as is the case with the opening of *Dog Day*. I suspect that the 'idea' for the opening was an afterthought — it does not unite, or contribute to the needs of the story.

HINT: It is an example of what comes of separating Place, Story, and Character. Perhaps the montage was constructed (so as) to make 'full' use of the accompanying Elton John song.

To juxtapose right — appropriately and effectively — it is necessary to understand, and to ultimately develop, a 'feel' for visual logic. Foremost is the **visual logic** that is inherent in any specific image — the meaning or feeling it stimulates.

There is a good 'workout' I often employ, and recommend to students. It came about as a result of my "Philadelphia, West Virginia Bacon incident."

I ask the students to take note of image(s) impressions, and any resulting assumptions. This is particularly helpful, when they later 'learn' that they were misled, confused, or inaccurate. The idea is to become — as quick as the eye — sensitive to associations derived from any single image; and especially to combinations, distributions, and settings of images. The 'stay alert training' makes them more receptive, and insightful in their editing while, at the same time, it supplies consumer safeguards. Television is a good 'gymnasium' for the 'workout.'

The most fascinating feature of television is its never-ending juxtaposition of images: Putting aside advertising strategies in product appeal and sale — for a moment — what feelings, impressions, or assumptions are derived via all of the (unintentionally (?) edited) nonstop juxtapositions? Two of the infinite possibilities viewed, and noted, in my living room: captured Nazi film images of the Warsaw Ghetto Uprising, and a (next) commercial break: "Becks! Germany's Favorite Beer." And! An evening news account of starvation in Biafra — established by a film clip of a protein-deficient child, oblivious to swarming flies about his eyes — followed immediately (juxtaposed) with a 30-second 'breakfast' commercial: Special K! "You Can't Pinch An Inch On Me."

Madison Avenue thrives on knowing response probabilities to word and picture stimuli — they do lots of testing. An article in *National Geographic: The Science of Things* revealed that with "tens of millions of dollars spent to make and air ads," researchers "have spent decades watching people watch ads." Of particular interest: What do we do with our eyes.

While responses to images and their influence on purchasing patterns might seem less than logical, they reveal a furtive language, which is 'translated' instantly in the subconscious mind, effecting an intense — and even intimate — emotional reaction. Advertisers make every effort to create juxtapositions that 'trigger' impulsive desires. We are all susceptible!

One day, as I drove home from the supermarket, I laughed at myself. Why had I purchased bacon? I could only dimly recall taking the "West Virginia Bacon" from the meat case, and putting it into my basket. What was it that led me to believe

— gave the impression — that anyone in West Virginia would make uncommonly fine bacon? Was this the 'marketable' result of singer and songwriter John Denver?

I remembered that suddenly one semester, students began returning to the editing room — after our mid-class break — with Arizona Iced Tea. I wondered then what Arizonans knew about iced tea. I for one would have been more certain about North Carolinians. I made mental note! It turned out Arizona Iced Tea was bottled (at least back then) in Brooklyn, New York.

The moment I arrived home I looked through the grocery bags to find the bacon. The label did not say West Virginia Bacon. It read:

WEST VIRGINIA

STYLE

BACON

When I turned the package over I laughed some more. The 'irresistible' bacon was smoked in Philadelphia, PA.

My 'bringing home the (Philadelphia, West Virginia) bacon,' and the students swigging down Brooklyn, Arizona Iced Tea, have led me to a lifetime investigation of visual logic — and to this chapter.

A working knowledge of visual logic is compulsory if the editor is to avoid baffling confusions.

You'll easily 'see' the puzzlement produced by visual *illogic* in the Sheriff Drives Mrs. Watts to Her Childhood Home scene from *The Trip to Bountiful*. A Close Up of the Sheriff and Mrs. Watts in the Sheriff's car, moving screen right to left, cuts to a Long Shot of a car traveling in the 'same direction' — screen right to left — 'pulling' into town. [*Figure 6.3*] We are instantly mystified when the driver and passenger exit...

Figure 6.3

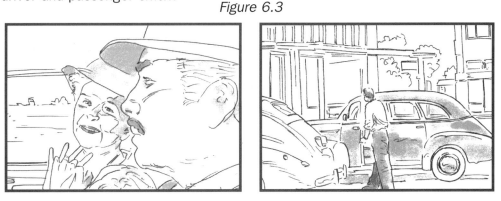

...This isn't the Sheriff and Mrs. Watts?

No! It's Ludie — Mrs. Watt's son — and his wife Jessie Mae, arriving at the Bus Depot from which Mrs. Watts and the Sheriff departed earlier. It is interesting that though the cars are different colors, this fact doesn't lessen the mix-up: Visual illogic is a persuasive trickster of false impressions.

Visual logic can be a compelling, 'naturally-descriptive' editing solution!

The cut, which follows Ludie and his wife's arrival at the bus depot, takes us behind the Sheriff's car as it drives down a country road, away from the camera — and away from the scene! Visual logic would have been (better) served if this image had come before the Long Shot of Ludie's car. [*Figure 6.4*] The Sheriff's car, moving away from the camera, visually and logically, would 'conclude' the Sheriff and Mrs. Watts scene.

Figure 6.4

Visually Logical in Place and Time

There is visual logic that influences dramatic structure. A good example comes from an SVA thesis film: *The Painter.*

A young man — a struggling writer — working as a freelance house painter, accepts a job in a beautiful — and expensive — Manhattan apartment owned by a career woman who will be 'out of town.'

Work begins! The painter 'listens in' as the woman's answering machine records messages from several suave men. He 'checks out' her photo album, admiring pictures from exotic vacation sites. He uses her CD player to enjoy selections from her music library, and he browses her 'coffee-table books' — one in particular catches his eye: recipes from Tuscany!

As the week of painting progresses the young man becomes ever more captivated by the woman. The young man becomes overly familiar [*Figure 6.5*]; his impetuous, and decisive actions — as scripted — were assembled:

1. Uncovering the woman's bureau from beneath a plastic cover.
2. Looking through the bureau drawers, and 'fondling' her most intimate items.
3. Going into the bathroom to peruse potions and lotions in her medicine cabinet.
4. Undressing, and getting into her 'luxuriously' foamy tub.

Figure 6.5

Visual Instinct is more than meets the eye

The Painter
Director, John Kelleran; Editor, Fanny Lee

After a 'last look' screening of *The Painter*, I told the student director, and editor, that I felt 'something' was off — as in amiss, faulty. I 'felt' it, and I trusted the feeling, but I didn't know exactly what it was. I asked the students to "Let me 'live' with the scene for a while."

On my way home — my NJ Transit commute — it 'clicked.' [*Figure 6.6*] The 'trouble' was in the sequential order of the young man's intrusions! I felt that #3 (perusing the medicine cabinet) would be better first. #1 and #2 (uncovering the bureau and handling intimate items) would be better positioned #2 and #3, so that, following the young man's gentle and sensual touching of the woman's silk undergarments and other suggestive belongings, a cut would take us to #4 (undressing and bathing).

It seemed to me that going into someone's bathroom, and looking into — even through — her medicine cabinet, is far from uncommon. It's likely a tolerable act of voyeuristic license. It's certainly not as excessive as handling someone's personal apparel, and bubble-bathing in her tub. Its (near) acceptance 'reduced' the dramatic lure of the scene(s). The new order would intensify the dramatic force of the scene(s) with a visually logical order to the young man's audacity.

Figure 6.6

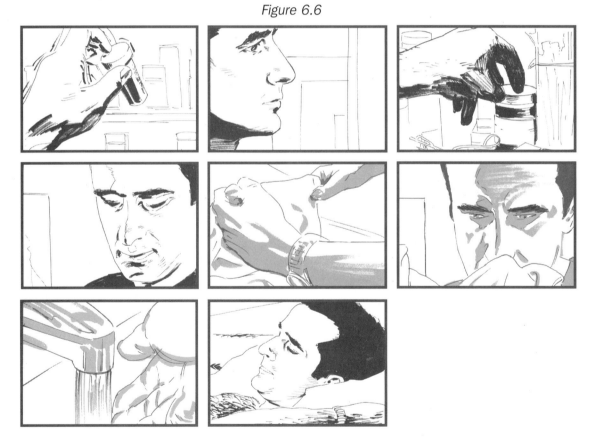

Showing more & more & more bravado

HINT: Visual Logic is a link to choices in the **Distribution of Information**; and in *The Painter* an example of an asymmetrical solution: The Bathroom scene became scenes.

There is Visual Logic that is fashioned by the selected moment of a cut. This model is especially useful when two relatively similar compositions are joined. The closer two compositions — especially in near matching scale — are to each other, the more difficult it is to join them with a cut that 'feels' right: The eye is quickly aware of an 'inadequate', or not-so-required 'new' image.

TIP: You can shape the success of such a join by 'giving motivation' to the moment of the cut. If something additional, or new, is disclosed within a very short span of time — 8 to 12 frames — the eye is satisfied with the new, though nearly identical, composition. In other words, the 'right' timing (beat) — especially of the Incoming shot — produces the visual logic.

A good example of this can be seen in the 'Popeye' Doyle, Russo, and Suspect in a Vacant Lot scene, from *The French Connection*. [*Figure 6.7*] In an Extreme Long Shot the suspect is dragged, thrown to the ground, and kicked. A cut takes us to another Long Shot — for large screen presentation it represents but a slight difference — barely a beat before Russo hauls the suspect off the ground. The 'haul-up' — quickly following the Incoming cut — is new, and creates visual logic by giving 'motivation' to the Incoming shot.

Figure 6.7

A Beat of Visual Logic

HINT & TIP: This concept links ideas in the chapter "Mind Watching The Cut," and it is another way to attain an inconspicuous cut.

Beware the editing hazards of Dialogue Scenes: The order and meaning of the spoken word — a more familiar kind of logic, verbal logic — must not distract you from the visually (logical) dramatic needs of a scene.

No matter how 'sound' — and even logical — the order of dialogue, it was first written to the requirements — and demands — of a screenplay. The editing opportunities will not be fully apparent until the script is brought to film, and the combinations in image and sound are far more malleable than you're likely to guess.

HINT & TIP: The editing and re-editing process can permit startlingly better — visual and verbal dramatic logic — possibilities.

The eyes of characters — available after filming — have a good deal to do with this. The 'Popeye' Doyle and Russo 'Rough Up' a Suspect scene from *The French Connection* — described in the chapter "Editing With Two Left Feet" — makes that clear. [*Figure 6.8*] Physical impossibilities in 'real life' become visually 'acceptable' — logical — in film; especially possible if the order of cuts is allied to the attention (focus) in a character's eyes.

Figure 6.8

Visual & Verbal Logic: The EYES have it!

Visual logic is indispensable to avoid the (all too often) randomness in the order of shots in a dialogue scene. It may not be the cut itself, but the 'joined' compositions that are (too) apparent, and jarring. Cuts from Long Shot to Close Up to Medium Shot, and every possible permutation of every possible composing, requires a decent consideration of visual logic, even when the dialogue follows in (more or less) verbally logical order.

TIP & HINT: There is a limit to the number of set-ups that can be employed successfully in any specific scene. After that point is reached the cuts are harmed by sheer chaos to the eyes.

For a chance to 'see' a conspicuous example of arbitrary joins — too many set-ups — that produce strong visual illogic, screen the Bus Depot Clerk and Mrs. Watts scene from *The Trip to Bountiful*.

Medium Shot of Mrs. Watts: From behind, and over the left shoulder of the Clerk.

MRS. WATTS
(putting down her small suitcase)
...just to stand on the porch of my own house again.

Cut to: Medium Shot of the Clerk: From behind, and over the right shoulder of Mrs. Watts.

CLERK
Lady I don't have anything....

Cut to: Medium Shot

MRS. WATTS
(interrupting)
I thought last night that I had to stay....

Cut to: Medium Shot of the Clerk

MRS. WATTS
(continues)
...I thought I'd just...

At the moment of this Outgoing cut, the Clerk turns to screen left. We get a "mental hiccup," as our eyes follow the movement of the Clerk's face as the Incoming cut takes us to:

Close-Up of Mrs. Watts

MRS. WATTS
(continues)
...die. I couldn't stay. But now I'll settle for less.

The eye/brain is startled by the "mental hiccup," but also by the choice of beats — they do not motivate a cut — and by the arbitrary, and visually illogical combining of images. The Close-Up of Mrs. Watts seems to come out of nowhere; because, visually, it does! [*Figure 6.9*] There is little visual logic to the order of the set-ups — and a resulting conspicuousness in the number of set-ups.

Figure 6.9

Fewer set-ups might afford a little Visual Logic

During Mrs. Watts' last line she moves forward — Physical Action — to the camera, and the Clerk. Her stepping forward — if seen in the Medium Shot — would have helped serve the visual logic of new, and tighter set-ups on Mrs. Watts and the Clerk.

Instead: A Cut takes us behind Mrs. Watts again, and we are very aware that now she isn't closer to the Clerk. [*Figure 6.10*] The visual logic 'says,' Mrs. Watts must have hopped back and away.

MRS. WATTS
An hour.

Figure 6.10

Concentrating on the order of dialogue is not enough

Another cut and we are back to the Close-Up of Mrs. Watts, and to visual illogic.

Mrs. WATTS
A half-hour.

From here, confusion in beats, and an eagerness to make things work, leads to harmful over-cutting.

The arbitrary structuring of images in a dialogue scene is not uncommon; it is usually insignificant — and goes unnoticed. It is seldom as evident as in *The Trip to Bountiful*.

TIP: With time, and experience, you will start to spot them when you're at the movies and — more important — in your own work.

Let me offer a few examples in the good use of Dialogue and visual logic.

Frau Mozart Seeks the Aid of Salieri scene, from *Amadeus*. The scene opens in Medium Long Shot:

SALIERI
(stepping forward)
How can I help you?

In Long Shot — which establishes the space between the characters — we see a woman, her face covered by a veil. She removes the veil. A cut returns us to the opening composing.

SALIERI
Frau Mozart?

A cut brings us to the Long Shot of Frau Mozart.

FRAU MOZART
I've come on behalf of my husband. I've
brought you some samples of his work,
so that he can be considered for the
Royal appointment.

A cut takes us back to Salieri. On his next line he steps forward, and toward Frau Mozart.

SALIERI
How charming. But why did he not come
himself?

HINT: Salieri's Dialogue, spoken as he steps — Physical Action — toward Frau Mozart, is an example of integrating (beats) elements.

Salieri comes to rest; a beat is held.
Cut to: A new composition. A Medium Shot of Frau Mozart.

FRAU MOZART
Well, he's terribly busy sir.

Salieri's Physical Action motivates a change in composition; [*Figure 6.11*] and the cut to a Medium Shot of Frau Mozart is neither arbitrary, nor visually conspicuous.

Figure 6.11

Doesn't this 'feel' naturally comfortable — Visually Logical?

Basil Pascali and Mr. Bowles Meet the Pasha scene, from *Pascali's Island*. The Pasha is not in his office when Pascali and Bowles arrive. In Long Shot Bowles sits at the Pasha's desk. Pascali looks out a window. A cut from this Long Shot takes us to — an Extreme Long Shot — Pascali's (POV) Point Of View into the courtyard below. 'We' see the Pasha, and his assistant, meeting with a German industrialist. A cut to a Medium Shot of Pascali — still looking out the window — carries us to Pascali's focus of attention. What occurs next is simple and lovely visual logic: While in this Medium Shot, Pascali leans ever so slightly forward — his face now closer to the window. A cut 'transports' us to a Medium Shot of the three men in the courtyard — we hear their dialogue. [*Figure 6.12*] Pascali moved closer to the window, and we, with visual logic, got closer to the three — and their words — in the courtyard below.

Figure 6.12

Film does not necessitate a Visual Reality

Next, an example of 'finding' a visually logical moment to cut from a Close-Up to a previous (Master Shot) Establishing Shot.

Basil Pascali and Bowles Quarrel About the Pasha's Lease scene, from *Pascali's Island*. A waiter carries a coffee tray away from the camera, and Close Up, into the Long Shot setting of a Turkish café. We follow the waiter; his arrival at a table takes us from this first shot, by way of a cut, into a Medium Long Shot. Pascali, and Bowles are seated at a table. This Medium Long Shot will be the new, and later reused, Establishing Shot in our example. Several beats pass:

PASCALI
I've been all over the town looking
for you....

We 'stay' in our Medium Long Shot (Establishing Shot) for Pascali's grave concerns about the Pasha's lease.

BOWLES
I'd like to leave it for a day or
two old chap.

Cut to: Close Up of Pascali

PASCALI
Leave it, but why?

The conversation continues with a 'back and forth' in Close-Ups.

BOWLES
You thought the whole thing was a
fabrication I suppose.

A cut takes us back to the Medium Long Shot (Establishing Shot). Pascali makes a waving gesture with his hand, [*Figure 6.13*] to emphasize:

PASCALI
I don't know. I don't know what I believe.
Why did you not make this clear before?

Figure 6.13

The wave of a hand; like Magic!

A new, and dramatic gesture — Pascali's hand wave — affords the editor a visually logical premise to cut back to the Medium Long Shot (Establishing Shot). The audience is contented — and visually comfortable — with the Establishing Shot; they are witness to a new gesture.

A HINT: This is comparable to the visual logic in the 'Popeye' Doyle, Russo, and Suspect in a Vacant Lot scene from *The French Connection* mentioned earlier in the chapter. The *Pascali's Island* scene occurs in a more traditional dialogue 'setting.'

It is equally important that a visually logical purpose gets us back to our Close-Ups. A touch in timing — a 'feel' that does come with experience — can supply the logic.

HINT & TIP: Nothing beats visual logic, and visual logic is often 'discovered' in the beats.

cutting
emotional
attachments

"Many (editors) have the technique. I
don't think there are quite as many who
can make a film purely emotional...."

— Carol Littleton

The editor is supplied four components. There is Picture and Sound. That makes two. There are two kinds of Picture and two kinds of Sound. There is Silent Picture, abbreviated as MOS: Mit Out Sound. Legend reports this as a smart-alecky mimicking of "without sound" spoken by a German director working in Hollywood. It caught on and continues to this day! MOS is an image photographed without simultaneous or synchronized sound recorded. There is Wild Sound: This is a recording not done simultaneously or synchronized to the photographed image. Customarily, Wild Sound is a production recording of all sounds except dialogue. This might include background ambiance (room tone), and a variety of location recordings, which might contain some specific sound effects.

There is Synchronized Picture and Sound: Picture and Sound photographed and recorded simultaneously, and in synchronization. The last two of the four components usually represent the dialogue portions of each day's filming. All of these unedited components are known as Dailies or Rushes: Picture and Sound provided from the original camera negative, and either 1/4" tape or DAT recording. The term "dailies" is commonly used in the United States, while "rushes" is preferred in England and other Commonwealth countries.

The first assembly of the selected takes — the initial choices in picture (Pix) and sound (Sd; Trk; or Sd Trk) — from the four components is fittingly called a 'rough cut.' Sync Picture and Sync Sound are merged with the MOS material, and (at times) with the Wild Track. Every film is edited with an arrangement of these components. As postproduction continues, other components are added: Picture and Sound effects; Titles and Credits; Music; Re-recorded Dialogue; Narration or Voice Over.

During my years of teaching, I've noted an editing practice characteristically used by students and young editors alike. When working with the synchronized picture and sound elements of a scene, they will promptly, and unhesitatingly, **intercut** between the speaking actors. There is a back and forth from one actor to the other... and back again. But, while they 'jump-right-in' and intercut the dialogue elements, they scarcely ever intercut the MOS selected takes. Each selected MOS take from the dailies appears in a single position within a scene. In other words, there is no back and forth between MOS shots.

I am using the term intercutting to mean the joining together of selected moments from one camera run (or shot) in a scene, with selected moments from another (or several other) shot(s) from the same scene. I am not referring here to **cross-cutting** or **parallel editing**: the joining or intermingling of shots from two or more scenes. This is the 'accepted' definition for all three terms — they are used interchangeably — but I make a distinction for intercutting in this chapter.

HINT: Distinguish parallel editing from cross-cutting in the next.

Suppose we have a scene of someone looking through a dresser drawer. The selected MOS shots include: [*Figure 7.1*] A Close-Up of the someone's face peering into the drawer with assorted shoulder and head movements, indicating probing gestures; a Close-Up view inside the drawer, showing hands searching items; and a Medium Shot of the someone entering a bedroom, opening a drawer and rummaging through it.

Figure 7.1

Three Shots = How Many Cuts?

Using the three shots, the student begins to edit the "Someone's Going Through the Dresser" scene. The student's completed MOS scene would most likely be:

1. M.S. bedroom.   2. C.U. someone's face.   3. C.U. drawer.

Or

1. C.U. someone's face.   2. M.S. bedroom.   3. C.U. drawer.

Or

1. C.U. drawer.   2. M.S. bedroom.   3. C.U. someone's face.

Or

1. C.U. someone's face.   2. C.U. drawer.   3. M.S. bedroom.

Or

Some other variation of one appearance per shot. Seldom will the structure result in:

1. C.U. drawer.   2. C.U. face.   3. C.U. drawer.   4. C.U. face.
5. M.S. bedroom.   6. C.U. face.   7. C.U. drawer.   8. C.U. face.

Or

Some other intercutting of the three MOS shots!

TIP: It is crucial that care be given not only to selecting the takes, but also and especially, the moments within each take to be used in the cutting of the scene: What is the expression in the face? What specifically are the hands doing? What details can be observed in the Medium Shot of the bedroom? What particulars do we see in each 'revisit' of a shot?

In most movements or actions, from subtle to extreme, there are subdivisions in which one gesture changes, and another begins. In the Close-Up of the face we might detect deliberation become serenity, become contemplative, become irritability. In the Close-Up of the drawer, we might view the hands pull the drawer open, see the hands inward-bound, begin to poke around; pause, grab for and clutch an item; fling the item aside, exit, and close the drawer. In the Medium Shot of the bedroom we might watch as someone enters, approaches the dresser, looks intently, cautiously opens a drawer, reaches inside, dips lower to get a better look, lifts items, tosses items, closes the drawer, pauses, turns, and leaves the bedroom. All of these many points, in the actions of each shot, are distinctive and include transitions. The transitions are moments of shifting expressions and/or gestures. The editor can 'fix' on which (beats) distinctive action — or actions — might be used to 'hold' the scene. A single action from the Close-Up of the face? Two actions from the Close-Up of the hands in the drawer? One, two, or three actions from the Medium Shot of the bedroom?

TIP & HINT: Catching a frame or two of a transition in the action, whether in the Outgoing or Incoming frames, could produce a "mental hiccup." The quick-eye watches ever more alertly when a transition from one action to a new action is set in motion. An ever so slight new action, in transition, abruptly clipped, will disturb the eyes. There is a need for a mindful response.

When arranged well, the back and forth — intercutting — demonstrates a remarkable paradox in film editing: Fewer cuts can be more conspicuous than many cuts. Or: More cuts can be far less evident than fewer.

HINT: Be careful with the multiplicity of compositions. Too many set-ups in a scene — not the number of cuts — can result in perplexing eye/brain adjustments that may demand a simplification — or a reconsidered pace.

For a superb rendition of intercutting, watch one of the early scenes in *Serpico*.

Serpico in the Emergency Room scene: [*Figure 7.2*] The scene is an intercutting of five shots which total sixteen cuts. Beginning with a Medium Close-Up of a sock coming off Serpico's foot, and ending with a Close-Up of his eye, the intercutting advances emotion as it leaves the 'sixteen fragments' behind; and it does something equally vital. It crafts the needs of the scene's context: Portraying professionals working quickly from experience and training; not an emergency room staff hurrying recklessly, and in panic.

Figure 7.2

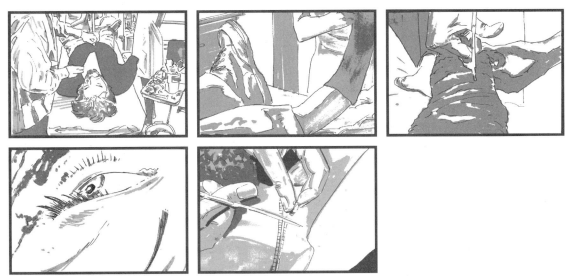

Five Shots = Sixteen Cuts

There is another moment within the scene worth mentioning. In Close-Up, Serpico's left shoe is taken off, and dropped. [*Figure 7.3*] Watch, and listen!

Figure 7.3

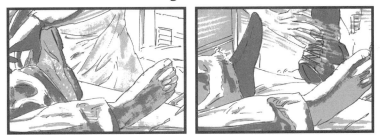

Where's the 'Clunk'?

The sound of the shoe hitting the floor is especially late; but only if measured against real time. It is just right when measured by the needs of the moment, and the next cut. If the 'clunk' were heard at exactly the 'accurate' instant, eyes and ears would be 'hit' concurrently, bringing 'too much' attention to the cut.

HINT: Here is another example where matching action — or matching synchronization — is neither necessary nor advisable.

Antoine Goes for a 'Spin' at an Amusement Park scene, from *The 400 Blows*: The scene, from Francois Truffaut's first feature film, intercuts three shots to make nineteen cuts. [*Figure 7.4*] The emotion produced by the choices, and timing, in the intercutting, guarantee that a smile will win your face, and...

Figure 7.4

...Centrifugal spirit will 'catch' your tummy

Walter Murch advises that emotion tops his list of six criteria that make for "the ideal cut." I think it is important to see that Murch's remark is not so much about the moment of a single 'splice.' It is instead a more expansive perspective: Intercutting is the surest way to a scene's emotion.

Murch also addresses the bias inherent in terminology. In the (United) States, film is "cut," which puts the emphasis on separation. In Australia (and Great Britain) film is "joined," with the emphasis on "bringing together." It is worthwhile to recognize this bias, and to keep in mind — and eye — that the editor's task is to 'separate' — as in 'to find' — the ideal moment(s) in any shot, and to 'join' them.

In "bringing (joining) together" the three MOS takes from the "Someone's Going Through the Dresser" scene, the editor isn't merely joining shots. By imaginatively and artistically *interjoining* facial expressions and hands from the Close-Ups, and body gestures and movement from the Medium Shot, the editor pulls together a wholly engaging scene. When this happens, however many the 'joins,' they will not be eye-stopping: An emotional attachment will have been crafted for the audience.

cuts
both
ways

*"...the film's dramatic requirements
should always take precedence over the
mere aesthetics of editing."*

— Edward Dmytryk

Editing is an inconspicuous art. It is not easy to be an artist, and inconspicuous. It is especially difficult to be young — an artist — and inconspicuous. There is an ongoing battle to be waged against the enticement to be conspicuous. The editor's ability to have the audience's eyes happily gripped by rapidly changing images, encourages the — young, or young at art — editor to over-cut; and this invariably leads to the (almost) 'sinful' — which likely adds to the temptation — overuse of cross-cutting and parallel editing.

Let me offer a distinction between the two terms. Cross-cutting — for me — is a better 'fit' to the traditional definition: the joining or intermingling of shots from two or more scenes. Parallel editing is better defined as: the joining of two or more scenes. It is a merging of fully intact scenes, and not, as in cross-cutting, the intermingling of individual shots from different scenes. Parallel editing is less 'flamboyant,' consequently less conspicuous, than cross-cutting; and far less likely to 'editorialize.' Cross-cutting or parallel editing excesses often result from efforts to 'save' an emotionally slumping scene, or sequence — or an entire film.

The classic use of parallel editing is often recognized in the opening to early moments of a film; with cuts between — sometimes among — diverse characters and/or places.

The French Connection opens in Marseilles, France. An undercover detective is on assignment: The scene in Marseilles leads to additional scenes, before the story takes us to Brooklyn, New York. There, two undercover detectives are on assignment: depicted in scenes. Parallel editing, in this format, assures a 'meeting' of the characters — eventually they do 'get together' in New York. For parallel editing to be (most) inconspicuous — for the technique, and process to avoid mere facade — it should do something more than 'perform' cuts between people and places. There should be a visual connection — though not necessarily French — between the characters and/or places. [*Figure 8.1*] In *The French Connection* we 'see' undercover detectives on assignment in Marseilles, and in Brooklyn.

Figure 8.1

VISUALLY Sharing

The opening of *Atlantic City* provides another classic example. We meet Sally in Atlantic City; and Lou is spying on her. Cut, and we meet Dave; he is spying a drug drop-off in a telephone booth in Philadelphia. [*Figure 8.2*] Both are intact scenes: There is no intermingling of shots as in cross-cutting.

Figure 8.2

They'll meet in Atlantic City. You can bet on it!

The 1989 release *sex, lies, and videotape* serves as an example of cross-cutting. It is also used at the film's outset, but here the technique is a 'flourish' of conspicuousness. [*Figure 8.3*] Graham 'is on the road' and is cross-cut with Ann, during her therapy session. The cutting is a 1:1 symmetrical — back and forth — intermingling of scenes.

Figure 8.3

Asymmetry would have cut the chaos

Given the context — Graham is already heading somewhere; to meet someone(?) — and no visual connection, it would have been less conspicuous, and more effective to 'stay' with Graham. Several imaginatively bold cuts of 'Graham's journey' would have been one of several better approaches. The editing's disjointedness is (especially) called to mind — and eye — by Ann's 'Voice-Over Discussion' with her therapist. The effort to link the scenes does the opposite.

HINT: An appreciation of context and simplicity is key.

Our prodigious attraction to tales — truthful and fictitious — seems certain to be of human inheritance. Søren Kierkegaard's comment that "Life can only be understood backwards, but it must be lived forward," instantly illustrates, and confirms, storytelling's appeal. The facility with which film can alter arrangements in Time, Place, and Character, makes parallel editing — cross-cutting still more — carelessly invigorating: They (can) so easily become the attraction, that the editor overlooks "the film's dramatic requirements."

Parallel editing can be effectively used throughout a film — not limited to openings. But great care must be taken to prevent the technique from becoming a leading indicator of film's episodic nature: You might find your work 'splitting' into a detectable visual schematic.

There are three categories of parallel editing:
1. TIME(S)
2. PLACE(S)
3. CHARACTER(S)

The French Connection and *Atlantic City* are — at their start — parallel edited PLACE. Inevitably, whatever the 'balance,' the categories operate in a configuration. Some configurations are more advantageous than others.

Catch-22 and *The Sweet Hereafter* are each structured in parallel edited TIME. [*Figure 8.4*] Since both have a principal character — protagonist — the otherwise 'debilitating' obviousness of the "mere aesthetics of editing" is happily reduced.

Figure 8.4

Catch-22

The Sweet Hereafter

Stories are, after all, about people

Iris is structured in parallel edited TIME. [*Figure 8.5*] It encompasses a lifetime. It is about people, but the observable *time design* takes its toll.

Figure 8.5

At some time, the Past Time should be left behind.

TIP: There often comes a time in a film when parallel edited TIME is no longer (as) effective. Consider staying (more or less) in a single selected TIME from that moment to the film's end.

CHARACTER(S) parallel editing is most ineffective when it 'plays' in a 1:1 ratio. That is, a continuous back and forth between CHARACTER(S), as if an Equal TIME Requirement were in effect.

HINT: Again, think asymmetry!

What is most precarious about the CHARACTER category is that it (often) lacks a clearly pronounced protagonist. A storytelling flaw: Whose story is it? Screen *The Big Chill* and/or *Laurel Canyon*. They become soap opera, exhibiting an edgy concern that all audiences are afflicted with Limited Attention Span Syndrome.

Cross-cutting is seldom a primary structural device, but often it suddenly materializes — delaying, or abandoning the story with a disruptive interlude. It 'spells out' themes; meanings; ideas; or propaganda. Screen the Czar's Soldiers Slaughter Workers and Butchers Slaughter Cattle scene(s) from *Strike*; and the Shaving Mister and African Pubertal Ritual scene(s) from *The Color Purple*. [*Figure 8.6*]

Figure 8.6

Strike

The essential measure of inconspicuousness requires that you do nothing more — or less — than stick to the story.

The Color Purple

Editing should not be about editing

a wealth
of distributions

"*Every film should have a beginning, a middle, and an end. But not necessarily in that order.*"

— Jean-Luc Godard

One evening, as Christmas drew near, my wife asked our son to tell me about a wacky thing that happened to him. At the time our son was a Special Ed teacher in New Jersey. He also had an after-school job at Monmouth Mall. A close friend's father owned a stationery store, and our son helped out. During that afternoon he had driven his car to Neptune, some fifteen minutes south of the mall, to pick up a carton of Zippo lighters to be displayed for Christmas sale. On his return, our son parked his car several dozen yards from the mall entrance, lifted the carton out of his car's trunk, and carried the Zippos to the store inside. Ten minutes later, over the mall's PA system, he heard this announcement: WILL THE PERSON WHO OWNS A RED (that's his car's color) NISSAN (that's his car's make) SENTRA (that's his car's model) WITH NEW JERSEY PLATES BXS867A (That's his CAR) COME OUT TO THE PARKING LOT TO RETRIEVE YOUR VEHICLE!

Our son hurried outside. He could see his car. It was more than 200 yards from where he had parked it, sitting in the roadway that circled the mall, close to a chain link fence that separated the roadway from a culvert and woods.

When he left his car he had not engaged the emergency brake, and the standard transmission was in neutral. The car had rolled backwards through the steeply sloped parking lot. Miraculously, it missed hitting any of the many light towers, other cars, holiday shoppers, and a UPS truck approaching the mall with a delivery. Several construction workers tried — but failed — to stop the car as it rolled past them at a curbside work site. They were waiting with the car, directing traffic around it.

During the next weekend, my wife and I had friends visit for dinner. My wife began to tell them about our son's close calamity. After furnishing background about the Zippo lighters, and our son's drive to Neptune, my wife revealed that our son had not engaged his emergency brake, and that, as he carried the Zippo carton to the mall, "His car started rolling through the parking lot...." I interrupted, contending that she was spoiling the story by tipping off our friends about the emergency brake, and by not holding back the other particulars until after the PA announcement, and our son's rushing out to retrieve his car. My wife and friends glowered at me. I apologized.

The evening provided many lessons. First of all, there is something to be said for good manners. Our friends were not expecting to hear about "The Monmouth Mall Incident" in the most resourcefully dramatic fashion, but rather in the pleasures of a civil setting. Respect required that the storytelling be accepted, without debate on the principles of storytelling excellence. I had been rude.

Sometime later I considered objective and subjective perceptions about storytelling — or story*showing*. How does the setting of presentation 'control' and dispense the showing and telling? Is superior storytelling nothing more than subjective judgment?

The answer to the second question seemed obvious. There must be an objective evaluation of good storytelling. We all know people with a knack for setting and arranging yarns in stunning display: friends who have a way with telling jokes. When Sam O'Steen was asked what he thought makes a good editor he replied, "Someone who can tell a joke… the timing's right and he tells just enough."

Finding answers to the first continue to hold my interest.

HINT & TIP: Sometimes the best story*showing* can be established through storytelling. Not in the technique and style of great oral tradition — I'm not talkin' Garrison Keillor, or my efforts at "The Monmouth Mall Incident" — but in a crisp, clear, and focused approach.

David Mamet gives a clear — and simple — example of this in *On Directing Film*: "The movie… is much closer than the play to simple storytelling. If you listen to the way people tell stories, you will hear that they tell them cinematically. They jump from one thing to the next, and the story is moved along by the juxtaposition of images — which is to say by the cut. People say, "I'm standing on the corner. It's a foggy day. A bunch of people are running around crazy. Might have been a full moon. All of a sudden, a car comes up and the guy next to me says…."

A thesis student opened his film, *Life Before Me*, with a Medium Close-Up of a young man gazing outward. Behind him, upper floors of buildings revealed that he was on a rooftop. A series of shots 'saw' him open an envelope; read a letter; bow out of frame; untie his shoes; take them off; and climb onto the roof's ledge.

I asked the student to tell this opening scene in the order of his cuts. "A young man is on a roof. He reads a letter. He unties his shoes. He takes them off…." [*Figure 9.1*] I asked how it 'sounded' this way: "Someone is untying his shoes. He takes them off. It is a young man. He is on a roof…." [*Figure 9.2*] We agreed on the second version.

Figure 9.1

This…

Figure 9.2

…became This

Life Before Me
Director, Chris Graham; Editor, Ian Brownell

This simple device is what helped to 'find' the opening arrangement for *Serpico*. The original opening followed — as scripted — a chronology, which began with the commencement, and graduation from the Police Academy. An energy and urgency was missing, and, it was agreed, very much needed. So, in place of: [*Figure 9.3*] Here is the Police Academy graduation; here is Frank Serpico; here is his happy and proud family; here is his first day on the job, a new opening emerged. [*Figure 9.4*] Who is this scruffy guy with blood all over his face? This guy is in a police car, and he's a cop? Another cop could have shot him? The *New York Times* knows this guy? The audience can't help but get caught-up in this new showing.

Figure 9.3

This...

Figure 9.4

...became This!

Let's examine the Distribution of (so very much) Information in Jerry Meets Carl and Gaear in the Saloon scene from *Fargo*. In (nearly) obvious — and implausible — exposition we learn that Jerry is hiring the two to kidnap his wife; for a split of the ransom; which will be collected from his father-in-law; who is wealthy; but doesn't like Jerry; who needs money; because he's in some kind of trouble. [*Figure 9.5*] The next twenty minutes (or so) of the film is 'dedicated' to a distribution of information which verifies that Jerry did not lie to the kidnappers. Thin — and pointlessly redundant — story cargo; unless Jerry's 'story' was, at least in part, a lie.

Figure 9.5

A 'Telltale' Scene

What if we had only heard something about 'a ransom?' What would the next twenty minutes 'conserve' for the audience? What if the audience thought that Jerry might be 'plotting' the kidnapping of his father-in-law? What if this scene were (much) later? What if this scene were deleted?

HINT & TIP: Ask a whole bunch of questions!

If "The Monmouth Mall Incident" were 'told' on film, other possibilities in presentation would have to be considered. The selecting and ordering of information is fundamental to good storytelling. The primary distinction between poor storytelling and good storytelling is in the distribution of information.

If, in the telling of "The Monmouth Mall Incident," my wife had withheld information about the emergency brake, an important part of the punch in the story would have been preserved for a more advantageous moment. But, if my wife were showing "The Monmouth Mall Incident" as in an edited film, the emergency brake information might be one of the 'punches' to exploit earlier:

EXTERIOR. MONMOUTH MALL. DAY.
A RED NISSAN SENTRA pulls into a parking space. A young man gets out, and walks to the back of the car. He unlocks the trunk. The young man lifts a carton from inside the trunk. He slams the trunk closed, and carries the carton toward the mall.

In our film version of "The Monmouth Mall Incident," we could 'show' an Extreme Close-Up of the emergency brake. It is not pulled up. Or we might 'show' a Close-Up of one wheel. Perhaps we see the wheel begin to roll. We might hear 'creaking' while we 'show' the Extreme Close-Up of the emergency brake; the sound precedes a cut to a wheel. The audience 'sees' it begin to roll.

In this presentation, letting the audience know something that the young man doesn't, might prove emotionally beneficial to good storyshowing. [*Figure 9.6*] Here, the distribution of information is making use of:

Figure 9.6

Dramatic Irony

The Audience knows something our son doesn't

Dramatic irony can help deliver tension, conflict, humor, emotional fervor, and above all, an eagerness to 'see' what the story will bring.

Playwright Tom Stoppard presented a superb example of how the distribution of information — utilizing dramatic irony — influences the lot of storytelling. A man and woman are on stage. The setting is a living room. The man stands before a small bar. "Would you like a drink?" he asks. "That would be nice," answers the woman. The man fills two glasses from a whiskey bottle, and hands a glass to the woman.

Not much of anything here; even trite. But, what if the audience knows that the woman recently joined Alcoholics Anonymous? What if the audience knows that the man is a suspected poisoner? What if the audience knows that, earlier in the day, the man's roommate used the whiskey bottle for a urine sample? Mediocre scene now?

The raw stuff of the dailies prompts an exploration in arrangements, connections, and associations, that form an extensive 'balance' in the distribution of information:
    1. Dramatic irony.
    2. Insight(s) unknown to the audience, but possessed by a character.
       This requires 'indication.'

A splendid example appears in *The Verdict*: [*Figure 9.7*] Attorney Frank Galvin is about to give up ever locating a missing witness. He opens a can of beer, takes a nip, and puts the can under his chin. He 'holds' it there as he sorts through the day's mail, which includes his New England Telephone Company bill. Galvin looks intently at the envelope. He eases the can out from under his chin!

Figure 9.7

Galvin knows something! The Audience doesn't, but wants to!

    3. Insight(s) gained simultaneously by audience and character.

HINT: These are three of nine key elements.

It is essential to recognize that there is a considerable difference between the audience not having all of the information — yet enthusiastic to go on with the story — and an audience befuddled.

The postproduction exploration into the distribution of information was summed-up vividly by one of my thesis students: After many months of intense work on his feature length project, he announced, "I've come to realize that my screenplay only got me my dailies. I still had to find my film."

TIP & HINT: 'Finding' a film demands a readiness to shuffle scenes; and this directs the editor to a rearrangement of sequences.

zoom-in from the cosmos

"To teach is to learn twice."

— Joseph Joubert

Teaching film editing has made me more attentive to the overall progression of the filmmaking collaboration than if I'd simply worked as a film editor. It has made me aware of 'misleading' terminologies.

The term Master Shot communicates immense importance and worth. The term Cut Away/Insert communicates slim value. Yet their concrete significance is lopsided. The Master Shot might well 'play' an entire scene, but it is fundamentally a paradigm of theatre — and all too frequently 'opens' every scene in a screen-play. The Cut Away/Insert is often considered a 'piece of protection' permitting the editor to 'get out of trouble' by using it in brief, then to return to the 'real shots' of the scene. It is of far more value; and seldom mentioned in a script.

The Cut Away/Insert is a Close-Up, or Extreme Close-Up, of a 'bit' of a subject, or an object. It is the fulfillment of the proverb, "A picture is worth a thousand words." It is, therefore, capable of swift, simple, and absorbing storyshowing!

A stunning example of such storyshowing from *The Verdict*: Galvin Confronts the Admitting Nurse scene. Attorney Galvin has been searching for a missing witness who can provide evidence on behalf of his client — a young woman given the wrong anesthetic during childbirth, and now in a permanent coma. He learns that the witness — the former admitting nurse — has left Boston, the place of the story, and is 'hiding out' in New York City. He flies to New York to seek her help.

With a Cut Away/Insert of a Boston to New York airline ticket in the breast pocket of Galvin's overcoat — spotted by the nurse — we know that she knows exactly what the 'visit' is about. [*Figure 10.1*] A thousand words in (dreadful) dialogue are avoided: Exposition, which would have 'forced' the audience to sit through a 're-telling' of events and information while the 'new arrival' in the film — the admitting nurse — gets 'caught up' on the background facts of the court case; and the attorney's introduction and request.

Figure 10.1

...And not one word more...

You will find mention of this scene — on the last page — in Ed Dmytryk's *On Film Editing*. He hoped it signaled a return to the montage approach to filmmaking. When montage is efficient — Cut Away/Insert assisted — it calls to mind the ancient, and original, adage: One picture is worth ten thousand words!

Awareness of how students, and those new to editing, begin to construct scenes — most conspicuous, film openings — directs me to this topic.

HINT: The premise of this chapter is indispensable to suggestions offered later.

It is easier to 'find' a scene by working from Close-Ups (Cut Away/Insert) Outward, than from Long-Shots (Master Shot) Inward. This approach, and structure, provides the audience with a "what will the story bring?" mind-set. Its helpfulness is obvious in the first cuts of a scene; its utmost value is observable in the opening of a film.

Most screenplays begin with a description of Place — an explicit Master Shot. This is often sustained in production, and frequently isolates Place, from Character, from Story. It is altogether enticing to begin a film with this (admittedly) exaggerated opening:

1.   The PLANET EARTH. Zoom-In to:
2.   The WESTERN HEMISPHERE. Zoom-In to:
3.   NORTH AMERICA. Zoom-In to:
4.   The UNITED STATES. Zoom-In to:
5.   The MIDATLANTIC STATES. Zoom-In to:
6.   NEW YORK STATE. Zoom-In to:
7.   NEW YORK CITY. Zoom-In to:
8.   A WINDOW In An Apartment Building. Zoom-In thru:
9.   The WINDOW To See Our PROTAGONIST.

Such a structure manufactures surplus beginnings while delaying the story. There is a kind of 'introduction' of elements: Here is the Place; here is the Protagonist — or other Character(s); now, let's start the Story. Simplicity — and good storyshowing — is better served when elements are integrated.

HINT: Add Place, Character, and Story to the three Distribution of Information elements from the last chapter. You now have six key elements.

For terrific examples of integrating Story, Place(s), and Character(s), screen the opening scene(s) in *Atlantic City* and *Chinatown*.

Atlantic City does not open with a panoramic view of Atlantic City, or a "Welcome to Atlantic City" sign. It opens on a Cut Away/Insert of lemons. [*Figure 10.2*] A knife cuts the lemons. A finger hits the play button on a cassette-radio. We see a woman wash herself with juice from the cut lemons.

Figure 10.2

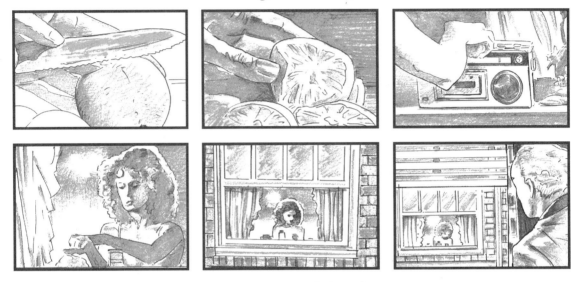

The camera moves Outward...

Chinatown does not open with a panoramic view of Los Angeles followed by a Zoom-In past an exterior Private Investigator sign, and into an office window. It opens on an Extreme Close-Up of a black-and-white still of a couple, surreptitiously photographed, in the act of lovemaking. [*Figure 10.3*] A hand sorts through additional photos. The camera moves Outward to reveal a second man — certainly the PI — seated at his desk, watching the man with the pictures: the PI's client, and cuckold.

Figure 10.3

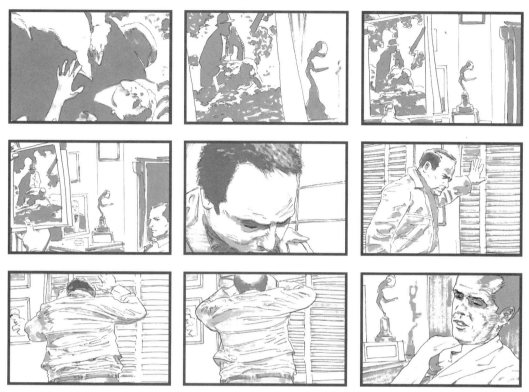

...Distributing ever-newer information

TIP & HINT: Both films use vivid and dramatic contrasts between Image and Sound.

In *Atlantic City*, cleansing the body with freshly squeezed lemon juice is accompanied by a recording — from the cassette-radio — of a Maria Callas aria. In *Chinatown* the photographs are accompanied by whimpering. What at first could be sounds of lovemaking ecstasy — coming from the still photos(?) — turns out to be the husband's suffering moans.

Good examples of openings that delay storytelling by ineffectively partitioning Place, Character and Story: *Joe Gould's Secret* and *Straight Story*.

Joe Gould's Secret introduces Place via 'Time.' [*Figure 10.4*] Precious time is taken-up with an introduction to era.

Figure 10.4

Don't make the STORY wait

Straight Story spends an exorbitant amount of Time on Place, [*Figure 10.5*] superfluously introducing the locale and 'settings,' then, (almost) Zooms-In and through a window.

Figure 10.5

Was I not exaggerating?

HINT & TIP: A Cut Away/Insert doesn't have to 'sit silently by.' It can be fully integrated with other images, and sounds.

For an example of a Cut Away/Insert brilliantly integrated — and intercut — with dialogue, and physical action, screen the Detective Comes Calling on Colin scene from *The Loneliness of the Long Distance Runner*. Money has been stolen from a neighborhood bakery. Colin is a prime suspect, and the chief detective on the case comes to 're-question' him. The scene takes place in the doorway of an English working class row house. A heavy rain is falling. [*Figure 10.6*] The stolen money 'washes' down, and out, from its hiding spot: the rain gutter's downspout.

Figure 10.6

A Cut Away/Insert beautifully incorporated

I would ask this of screenwriters, directors, and editors: What is the first shot? How does it fix Character, and Place, to Story? Does the first shot advance inquiry? Where are we? Who is this? What is going on?

OPENING SHOT: Extreme Close-Up. "ESCAPE" Key.
A FINGER enters the frame and hits the Key.

where'd the time go?

"As a loyal believer in the Auteur Theory I first felt editing was but the logical consequence of the way in which one shoots. But, what I learned is that it is actually another writing."

— Bernardo Bertolucci

A number of years ago I received a "Hello! Do you remember me?" letter from Germany. It was from a former Continuing Ed student. He was uncertain that I would, and he refreshed my memory by recounting one evening in the editing class.

Most Continuing Ed students arrive after a full day at work; at times they are weary on arrival, or will be soon. I try to provide a mix of hands-on editing, critique, screenings, and discussion in each and every class. This seems to revitalize the group.

Following a VCR screening of a film sequence, I put forward a few ideas about Time. Time — let's not forget beats — as it was represented in a scene; in a sequence; and its relation to the employment of time in the film's overall form. The student from Germany raised his hand.

First he mentioned a topic that I had discussed some classes back. The topic had to do with the two-dimensional presentation of film; apprehension stirred-up by the 180 Degree Rule — how to figure on what side of a scene to place the camera — and the possibilities for film to describe three-dimensional space; and the editor's place in all of this. The student asked, "Isn't this week's topic, 'Film Time,' actually the same as a previous topic, 'Film Space'?" Then he embarked on a crisp summary of Einstein's theory of General Relativity.

I'll keep this part simple. I try very hard to steer clear of theory, and I remind the reader that I don't do fractions.

The student's first-rate account of Einstein's ideas about space/time continuum did establish a number of principles which fascinatingly linked Einstein to film editing.

A screenplay — storytelling — and the production that depends on it, contains both Definite, and All-Purpose Time: A story might 'play' in a chronological Time Structure of a Definite day, or two, or three; or 'play' in a non-chronological Time Structure of All-Purpose days, or weeks, or more; or 'play' in a combination of time structures. It is not uncommon to discover that adjustments are required. Often conversions are necessary. The recognition that time shifts are desirable brings together the editor's search and Einstein's theory.

Albert Einstein put it like this: "When a man sits with a pretty girl for an hour, it seems like a minute. But let him sit on a hot stove for a minute — and it's longer than any hour. That's relativity."

Film Time is exactly what Mr. Einstein's example suggests: It is a feel of time; it is a sense of duration. It might be described as psychological time, or emotional time. It is why some 120-minute-long films seem interminable, while others of matching measured time seem fleeting. Most often it is not the quality of the story, but rather the qualities in the storyshowing.

1. *Alexander Nevsky*. The Battle on Ice scene. The Russian peasant army, under Prince Nevsky's command, awaits the German knights. The Russians stand (nearly) motionless. The German knights approach, at a gallop, across the frozen lake. [*Figure 11.1*] The prolonged tension is represented in the Time/Duration before the armies clash.

Figure 11.1

Extended Time;
Extending Tension

2. *Dog Day Afternoon*. Robbers and Hostages Exit the Bank and Board a Bus scene. [*Figure 11.2*] It takes longer (in measured time) for the robbers and hostages to make their way to the curb, and board the bus — there is visible repetition in the boarding actions — than it does to drive to Kennedy Airport. The Time Extension — and then Compression — underpins the dramatic storyshowing. Where is dramatic tension? How does Extending and Compressing Time enhance emotion as they move the story forward?

Figure 11.2

Editing Visual/Emotional Inflections

The *Dog Day* scene employs movement and motionlessness to produce Extended Time and Emotional Duration: the standing New York City Police officers and FBI agents, and the moving robbers and hostages. Some 40 years earlier the Nevsky scene did the same: the waiting Russian peasants, and the galloping German knights.

HINT, HINT: Contrasts in Juxtaposition.

3. *Witness*. The Amish Boy in the Train Station Restroom scene. Time is extended — many more toilets than earlier — as one of the killers searches the stalls looking for the source of a low cry. The Amish Boy escapes detection. The shot holds on his face. Beat, beat, beat. Then a cut: We see the back of a policeman.

We hear police walkie-talkies. The policeman clears the frame, and we see the Amish Boy in the arms of his mother. They are seated on a bench in the station waiting area. Policemen are all about. [*Figure 11.3*]

By 'passing up' images of the Amish boy 'screaming' out from the restroom, a brilliant instance of pure cinematic storyshowing is crafted:

Figure 11.3

The clout in Time Left Out!

"The hell of good screenwriting is that the most important part is what gets left out."

— Raymond Chandler

HINT & TIP: The Rhythm — in Image and Sound — that builds the killer's search of the stalls is (surprisingly) asymmetrical.

Let me point out a missed Time storyshowing opportunity in *Witness*. Gathering Amish make their way to a farmhouse. [*Figure 11.4*] A title appears:

Figure 11.4

Several scenes later, a horse-drawn carriage rolls along pristine countryside. In Long Shot, the carriage enters screen left; as it nears the midpoint of the frame, an '18-wheeler' approaches, air brakes sounding. [*Figure 11.5*] This shows us the way from the 19th to the 20th century.

Figure 11.5

Be careful with Pictured Words

A chief concern for the editor should be the correlation between the Time Frame of the story's events, and the film's Emotional Time. Simply, is it credible and effective for the events as structured to occur within the Time Frame of the story? The editor must fuse the distribution of information, and the 'feel' of Time.

TIP: There are always improvements in time structures to be uncovered in post-production. There are always time deletions to be discovered. A vital share of good storyshowing goes to Structuring Time.

A thesis student submitted a script. The story was classic in its premise, themes, and hopefulness. It derived many essentials from *The 400 Blows* and *The Bicycle Thief*. It was a tender tale of a mother and son facing great hardship in the aftermath of the father's death. Upon completion of a first assembly we screened *Dead End*. The assembly matched the sequential order of the screenplay — which read just fine — and we'd run into a problem. The Emotional Time felt too abbreviated, too hurried.

HINT & TIP: Everything changes when images are the means of presentation. The 'means' determine selection and arrangement.

We realized that we had to 'find' a configuration of images that would achieve a credible and effective presentation in storyshowing Time. The death of the father compels the mother to seek employment. In the screenplay, the descriptions of the mother's preparations to find work — looking in the classified section of a newspaper; checking her resume; dressing; applying make-up; going on interviews — were written for a single day. In the editing we separated these images to provide more (emotional) time. Instead of playing the Definite Time of one day, an All-Purpose Time of about a week was established. It was 'suitable' to have the mother wearing — in the dailies she was — the same clothing whenever she went job hunting: The 'outfit' was her finest. [*Figure 11.6*] The additional time was also good for the drama. The mother was more despondent after many days of failing to find work.

Figure 11.6

Dead End
Director, Bao Vu; Editor, Magnus Akten

The son has a severe limp, and is the target of a bully. When he leaves for school, he's stalked by the bully. Later, in the classroom, the bully continues his harassment. As written, the two events occur in the above order, signifying the Definite Time of one and the same day. In editing they were made to play as All-Purpose days by simple reordering. The bully is first encountered in the classroom scene....and on another day the son is teased on his way to school. [*Figure 11.7*] The street encounter is more perilous — the audience now knows the bully — and a freer, more expansive 'feel of time' is established.

Figure 11.7

No Continuum; More All-Purpose Time

In the screenplay the mother has little money left in her checking account, and lots of bills to pay. When the landlord threatens eviction, and sexually propositions her (in the presence of the boy), she takes the boy's watch — a prized gift from the father — to a pawnshop for quick cash. In the screenplay the son applies for a job as a restaurant delivery boy; he is turned down for want of a bicycle. He steals one!

These events were reordered: We see the mother with bills. The watch is brought to the pawnshop. [*Figure 11.8*] The quick cash will pay the bills. It is several days — and job searches — later that the landlord threatens eviction, and makes sexual advances, in the boy's presence.

Figure 11.8

The pawnshop cash is 'now' only a temporary solution for the family

Many days and events have passed since the boy sought the restaurant job. Only now does the boy steal a bicycle. [*Figure 11.9*] Good for the drama: The boy must make money to defend the honor of his mother; the audience feels ambivalent.

Figure 11.9

Stealing is wrong, but...?

Also reordered was the screenplay's scene of the boy's single day on the job — the same and definite day the bike's owner shows up. We increased the feel of time by separating specific actions: the boy with his bike arriving at the restaurant following a delivery; exiting the restaurant to make a delivery; inside the restaurant, getting paid, and counting his money; returning home, and hiding the stolen bike. [*Figure 11.10*] This last appeared in the screenplay immediately — Definite Time — after the boy stole the bike.

Figure 11.10

All-Purpose days at work

The new structure provided a far better distribution of event, consequence, and (attempt at) solution. It engendered a brazen dilemma for the boy, and considerable despair for the mother. It strengthened the drama. It readily, and strikingly, established a credible and effective Duration — a feel of time.

HINT & TIP: Screen The Captain and Dersu Explore a Frozen Lake scene from *Dersu Uzala*. Take note of the entrance and exit beats of the men at cut points. Some depict the two already in frame — sometimes walking; other 'times' still. [*Figure 11.11*] The scene is a masterful example of creating — in measured minutes — hours of escalating fear.

Figure 11.11

HINT: A study in Asymmetrical Beats

While it is possible to 'cut and paste' script pages to find new structures, the logic of words is unlike visual logic. It is why, once the dailies are in, many editors no longer care to 'look at' the screenplay. Visual logic will stir generous transformations — many not perceptible in the script reading. The possibilities are vast, and clearly 'pictured' when the film is viewed, assembled, and viewed again. Scenes unexpectedly connect in new assortments, building new — and resourceful — Sequences.

The re-editing of *Dead End* changed an ineffectual three Definite Days into a strong emotional duration of All-Purpose weeks. Yet, with simple Einstein magic, the film's running time remained the same!

influence
of sphere

"The most beautiful thing we can experience is the mysterious. It is the source of all true art and science."

— Albert Einstein

Einstein treasured simple solutions to make clear the mysterious. I think it would have delighted him to interpret the 180 Degree Rule. This rule is usually the first specification that film students learn. While content to hear 'rule' — it can be a support — students fear defying its 'warning'; they are cruelly paralyzed by its conditions. What is this Rule? How might the undaunted Einstein move filmmaking into unrestrained space?

Think back to your earliest drawings. Landscapes were the most popular for me. The top of the paper was reserved for the sky, clouds, and sun — I don't remember ever drawing a moonlit scene. The bottom was reserved for grass and trees. On the table-top-like ground I would draw a house. [*Figure 12.1*] The entire drawing signaled a world in two dimensions.

Figure 12.1

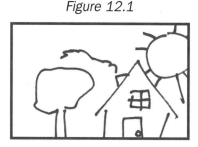

Then came a breakthrough...

I learned the fundamentals of vanishing point perspective. I would place a dot in the center of the paper. From the bottom edge I would draw two lines, beginning several inches from each other, which 'met' at the dot. This would create a roadway traveling 'into the distance' of the paper. By moving the dot higher or lower from the bottom edge of the paper, or by drawing the two lines closer or farther apart, I could create a bird's eye, or ground's eye view of my roadway. [*Figure 12.2*]

Figure 12.2

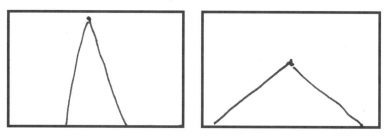

There was still more to learn...

If I drew horizontal lines attached to the roadway, I could create railroad ties — the train tracks moving 'into' the paper's distance. Turn the paper on its side, and the railway became a fence. [*Figure 12.3*] This three-dimensional illusion captivated me.

Figure 12.3

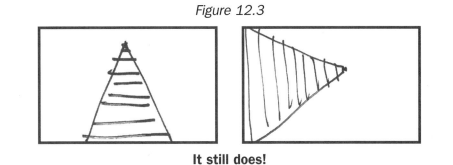

It still does!

Film images are recorded on a 'flat' strip of celluloid-triacetate. While the images depict our three-dimensional world, and this depiction — as was your earliest exploration of spatial illusions in your childhood drawings — is crucial to the eye-engaging aspects of motion pictures. Film is presented in two dimensions. It is projected onto a two-dimensional screen — structured in cuts — and the relationship of character, object, and place can be restrictively and puzzlingly cramped; or, it can be extra-roomy.

HINT: Remember the discussion about frame scope? Top and Bottom, Left and Right in "Editing With Two Left Feet"? The Left and Right of the film frame readily and naturally define the 180 Degree Rule.

I think the best way to begin to understand the 180 Degree Rule is to screen a scene that is faulty — spatially bewildering — and unnecessarily 'breaks' the Rule.

Macon Delivers a Letter to Muriel scene from *The Accidental Tourist*. Macon attempts to slip a 'Dear Muriel' letter under her front door. Muriel surprises Macon, and opens the door. Although Muriel and Macon are supposed to be facing each other, we see both facing screen left. [*Figure 12.4*] How this happens in production is simple, and best explains the configuration of the 180 Degree Rule.

Figure 12.4

How did this happen?

When actors face each other — quite common in dialogue scenes — one will (and should) be facing screen Right, and the other will be facing screen Left. This is how the audience 'knows' that they are facing each other when only one actor appears on screen. This holds from absolute profile through all camera placements until a character is full face, eyes looking straight ahead. While actors face each other with a 'correct' Left and Right, the camera must 'hold' this Left and Right relationship as well.

In the Muriel and Macon scene the compositions were produced with set-ups to the outside of each actor's left shoulder; resulting in both 'looking' to screen left. After filming Geena Davis (Muriel) 'looking' to screen left, the camera should have (simply) been 'aimed' [*Figure 12.5*] at William Hurt (Macon) with a turn to the left.

Figure 12.5

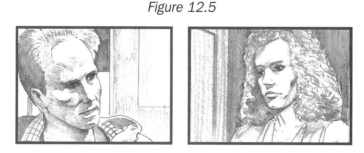

The way Macon and Muriel should be 'looking'

Instead, the shot of William Hurt was produced by moving the camera — and tripod — to the other side of the doorway.

HINT: To minimize the obviousness of the 180 break, the editing is judicious in its intercutting, and squanders several dramatic advantages — losing Emotional Attachments. Imagine the dramatic asset in seeing Macon while hearing Muriel open the envelope, and letter.

Yes, the camera can be moved all around the 360 Degrees of the production space, but the film is presented in 180 Degree segments. The order of these segments — cuts — should keep the spatial relationship(s) clear. Maintaining a 'correct' Left and Right is important to the visual logic of film's two-dimensional presentation.

Students will sometimes exclaim that they can "easily tell one character from another, even with a 180 Degree break," as if this were the central point of the visual logic to be considered. It isn't!

One Sunday morning I knocked on the front door of a friend's house. An elderly woman I had never met greeted me. She said, "Hello," and looked back into the living room. I leaned slightly to the right, and shifted my focus behind her. On the couch sat an elderly man I had never met. He did not look up, but continued to read his newspaper. The woman turned to me, and in a strong Eastern European accent added, "We are Sophie's parents. I am the momma" — she gestured toward the couch — "and that is the poppa."

TIP & HINT: Clear visual logic requires no verbal explanation.

I'm certain that if asked an audience could raise hands each (and every) time Muriel appeared on screen; and without any help — or hints — even I could have guessed the momma from the poppa.

At issue is the spatial relationships that occur when a 360 Degree Place — all locations — gets presented on a 180 Degree screen: Who is looking where? What happens when there are more than two characters? Who is looking at, or speaking to, whom? And, most important, how postproduction keeps all of this straight, while simultaneously bringing the audience from a proscenium presentation to a rich, and full — if only in illusion — three-dimensional place.

It is interesting that a related expression of visual logic was produced in the Macon and Muriel scene: The camera 'looks' slightly up at Muriel, because she is up a step inside the entranceway; while the camera 'looks' down to Macon. This visual logic 'softens' the 180 Degree break.

The principal reason that the 180 Degree Rule is confusing and inadvertently limiting, is that it is most often depicted in two-dimensions from above — a bird's eye view — but the Rule is of a Left and Right concern, not Top and Bottom. This common view 'fastens' the actors with a line — described as imaginary — and informs the filmmaker that no cut can be made which joins a shot taken from one side of this imaginary line, with a shot taken from the other. [*Figure 12.6*] This imaginary line with a warning not to 'pass the camera across' (by way of a cut) commonly describes the "Rule."

Figure 12.6

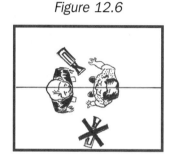

An imaginary line cuts space in half

This presentation is misleading at best, and incorrect in fact: An actor, turning to 'look elsewhere,' permits a 'cut across the imaginary line' [*Figure 12.7*] without breaking any "Rule…"

Figure 12.7

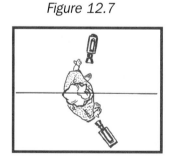

…and permits an exploration of the Space of Place

The possibilities that the 180 Degree Rule ought to encourage is best appreciated when the "Rule" is spatially depicted in the three-dimensions of the production space: with feet on the ground, and thoughts on a bow — as in bow and arrow.

Since Top and Bottom have nothing to do with our "Rule," let's position the bow parallel to the ground — its tips to the Left and Right. The arc of the bow corresponds to the many permissible (to hold to the "Rule") camera positions. The arc can be delicate or severe; the bow's length can be vast or teeny. [*Figure 12.8*] The string of the bow — the earlier imaginary line — is the link between subjects and/or objects.

Figure 12.8

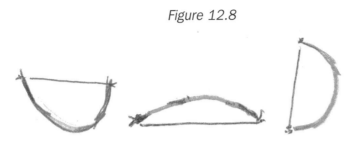

Let's move from the figurative to the "Rule's" practical application in directing, and the editor's obligation to 'find' an order — in cuts — which construct a full, and unambiguous, spatial field. Let's dwell in a roomy screen!

1. *Breaker Morant*. Who Do You Think Did Kill the Missionary? scene.
2. *The Verdict*. Pretrial Meeting in the Judge's Chambers scene.

The *Breaker Morant* scene opens in Exterior Long Shot. A stone wall crosses the entire frame — indicative of a two-dimensional point of view. The arc of the bow curves Outward to the viewer; the string of the bow links George Whitten to Peter Hancock. Pay attention to each character's Physical Action, and Physical Life: their movements in the space of the scene, and their engagement with objects. These elements prompt, and inspire, the fullness of the sphere to be realized. Whitten walks (Physical Action) from screen Right to Left; stops; and using a stone, inscribes his initials (Physical Life) on the wall. Hancock is crouched shining his army boots (Physical Life). A longer bow (and string) links Morant, who is in an open cell, lighting his cigarette (Physical Life). Morant exits the cell, and moves toward Whitten (Physical Action). Hancock stands in anger (Physical Action), throws his boots (Physical Life), and moves away from the wall (Physical Action). [*Figure 12.9*] The arc of the bow 'adjusts' its positions in a counter-clockwise 'swing' guided by the actor's focus of attention — eye contact.

Figure 12.9

All four points of a compass, without breaking the "Rule"

Concurrent with the 'adjusting bow,' the scene's Dialogue, Physical Action, and Physical Life are brilliantly engaged, and integrated.

TIP & HINT: Dialogue; Physical Action; and Physical Life are the last three of the nine key elements.

The scene demonstrates 'observance' of the 180 Degree Rule — and its spatial consistencies — while transporting the audience 'into' the 360 Degrees of the setting.

Interior scene from *The Verdict*: Frank Galvin, plaintiff's attorney; Ed Concannon, defendants' attorney; and Judge Hoyle, meet in the judge's chambers to 'negotiate a settlement.' Both attorneys are facing screen LEFT — 'looking' at the judge — and the judge faces screen RIGHT 'looking' at the attorneys. [*Figure 12.10*] Visualize the arc of the bow, and its string to 'see' how the 180 Degree Rule is easily maintained throughout the cutting.

Figure 12.10

Got your Settings?

In Medium Shot we have viewed Galvin, Concannon, and Hoyle from in front of each, with a sustained 'correct' Left and Right.

Let's move to the scene's most relevant spatial moment:

CONCANNON
Your Honor, Bishop Brophy and the Archdiocese
offered plaintiff $210,000.

JUDGE
What?

The next cut — back to Concannon — takes us slightly behind him. Note that he is still facing screen LEFT as he 'looks' to Judge Hoyle; [*Figure 12.11*] and the Judge still faces screen RIGHT to 'look' at the attorneys.

Figure 12.11

Left and Right still maintained

The bow, and its string which 'connects' Concannon and the Judge, holds the 180 Degree Rule. The bow, still held parallel to the ground with tips LEFT and RIGHT is now a Long Bow — at least a longer bow — with its Right tip passing Concannon's Left shoulder. This new composing on Concannon will present an opportunity to view the room beyond Galvin's Left shoulder: the fourth wall of the Judge's Chambers — unseen until now!

CONCANNON
My doctors didn't want to settle at any price.
They wanted this cleared up in court. They want
their vindication. I quite agree with them.
But for today the offer stands....

On Concannon's next phrase, "before the publicity of a trial begins," a cut to Galvin shows the last of the four walls: The bow is now behind the attorneys' chairs. Without breaking the 180 Degree Rule, Galvin and Concannon 'look' at each other in opposite screen directions [*Figure 12.12*] from earlier cuts: Galvin now 'looks' to screen RIGHT, and Concannon 'looks' LEFT.

Figure 12.12

What is the editor's part in all of this?

Here is the crucial moment in the continued integrity of the spatial relationship, while revealing the 360 Degrees of the judge's chambers:

CONCANNON
....so long as you understand that Mr.
Galvin. It's got to be that way.

On this phrase we see Galvin. [*Figure 12.13*] He turns to address Judge Hoyle.

Figure 12.13

GALVIN: We're going to try the case

Galvin looks to screen RIGHT when he addresses the Judge; and a cut to Judge Hoyle at this moment would have Hoyle looking to screen RIGHT as well, producing an unnecessary 180 break. The editor follows the cut of Galvin with a cut to Concannon [*Figure 12.14*] before a cut to Judge Hoyle.

Figure 12.14

A reaction cut to Concannon first, and we're home free!

Concannon's reaction not only serves the dramatic moment, its 'return' to the 'bow string' that linked the characters earlier maintains the 180 Degree Rule.

To see a (more than) 50-year-old wily solution to preserve the 180 Degree Rule, screen Dobbs Complains to Howard About Going for Provisions scene, followed by the Gila Monster scene, from *The Treasure of the Sierra Madre*.

A Close-Up of Howard from the Dobbs Complains scene is reused in the Gila Monster scene so as to cut to a Reverse Master Shot of Dobbs, Howard, and Curtain without a 180 break. [*Figure 12.15*]

Figure 12.15

Can you find it?

The most magnificently visual distinction between theatre and cinema is this exploration of space: to move the eye beyond a projected proscenium two-dimensional presentation, by way of the indispensable cut, into a wholly realized, three-dimensionally roomy screen.

all bets
are off

"The only person who behaves sensibly is my tailor. He takes my measure anew every time he sees me. All the rest go on with their old measurements."

— George Bernard Shaw

Stanley Kubrick said, "The truth of a thing is the feel of it, not the think of it." Great editors have a gift for getting at that truth: They 'feel' a fertile attachment to the material. They trust intuition, they allow intellect to flow from emotion, and they can 'feel' the difference.

In May 1994 editor Craig McKay attended the School of Visual Arts' Dusty Film Festival. He presented the award for Outstanding Achievement in Editing. In his opening remarks he said, "Editing is not an intellectual process. It's an emotional one."

This chapter is an intermission: a break from thinking. It is a disclaimer — a waiver from all I've expressed, and all you've pondered!

I offer a strong and certain caution: The truth cannot be shaped by a blend of editing 'ingredients.' Each time you work on a film you are obliged to unearth what it is about a moment, a scene, a sequence, and the entire form of that specific film that is 'one of a kind.' It is in the exclusive particulars — immense and trivial — that one finds the secret in any editing recipe: Context.

Context is why I don't do theory.

The *Howdy Doody Show* provided my introduction to Dramatic Irony. The show was among the early kid's programs on television. Howdy was a marionette dressed in western garb. He had a freckled face with a boyish grin. Buffalo Bob, a live jovial guy in a tasseled buckskin suit hosted the show, which featured the Peanut Gallery: a jury box of sorts, filled with a live audience of children. A cousin was scheduled to be a Peanut Gallery 'guest,' and all of the relatives — old and young — tuned in.

The cast of players included Clarabell, a mischievous clown. At some point during every show Clarabell would sneak up behind Buffalo Bob while he chatted with the kids in the Peanut Gallery. The kids could see Clarabell slowly approaching, always with a seltzer bottle. They shrieked, and motioned warnings to Buffalo Bob, who never seemed to understand the kids' hollering. "Having fun kids? Yes it's nice to see you all," he'd say with a 'missing the point' grin. Clarabell got closer and closer. The kids' squealing became frenzied. Buffalo Bob looked confused. "What? What is it kids?" He would finally turn, to see what all the ruckus was about. Clarabell would squirt him in the face with seltzer. The kids in the Peanut Gallery went out of control, some in laughter, some in frustration.

The kids on the show and the kids watching on TV always knew what Buffalo Bob never seemed to get. Dramatic irony added captivation and exhilaration.

Dramatic irony is the foundation of the storytelling in *Atlantic City*. As Sally learns — bit by bit — what the audience has already learned, the story unfolds.

Imagine in Karin and the Shepherds Picnic scene, from *The Virgin Spring*, if the audience didn't know that their encounter on the road was not a chance meeting, but was rather an ill-fated premeditation. [*Figure 13.1*] There would be a far less menacing discomfort.

Figure 13.1

The audience wants to shout a warning

We are 'feeling' context!

There is a moment in *Dog Day Afternoon* when the use of dramatic irony would be especially enticing: Unknown to Sonny and Sal the audience might see that the police are wise to the robbers, and are moving in. But! Dramatic irony is not used, with great result.

After several interruptions — which include several incoming phone calls — Sonny and Sal try to 'wrap up' their bank robbing work. The telephone rings again. The bank manager answers: He extends the receiver to Sonny, [*Figure 13.2*] "It's for you." The tongue-tied moment — an unhinged hush — is stunning. Sonny takes the phone...

Figure 13.2

..."Hello"?

On the other end of the line is a Detective Sergeant who announces that the robbers are trapped, surrounded by the police. Sirens and pandemonium let loose!

Did the dailies include footage of police officers 'sneakily' surrounding the bank to be used prior to the telephone call to Sonny — for the audience to see? I don't know, maybe not. It would still have been possible to use the existing material to allow the audience earlier knowledge of the police presence. In this instance, it was a terrifically smart decision not to use valuable, and (nearly) always effective, dramatic irony.

A long-established practice in editing supports the following principle — but only in theory:

    1. We see someone see something.
    2. We see what 'the someone' saw.
    3. We see 'the someone' react to what they saw.

This holds clear communication, and all the essentials of visual logic: In *The Verdict*, we see that the 'Admitting Nurse' sees something. We see the Boston to New York airline ticket in Attorney Galvin's overcoat pocket. We see the 'Nurse' react.

You cannot see a film that does not take advantage of this simple, and (nearly always) effective device.

But, what of Context?

In The School Bus Accident scene from *The Sweet Hereafter* we see the father driving his pick-up truck behind the school bus. His children wave to him through the rear window of the emergency door. He waves back. [*Figure 13.3*] But, instead of the expected 1, 2, and 3 we 'get' a 1, 3, and 2! We see that the father sees something. We see the father react, and only then do we see what the father sees.

Figure 13.3

Considering the context, a superior choice

HINT: Context connects to choices in the distribution of information.

One of the most common questions asked by students reflects an early editing challenge: "How long do I hold after someone leaves the frame, or before someone enters?"

Ed Dmytryk gives an answer, and justification: There is no reason to hold any frames after a character departs the frame. A simple and effective cut can (usually) be made before the last eye of the character is no longer visible.

HINT: Eye as Focal Point.

Dmytryk explains that a 'familiar' place — the Outgoing scene — is of no more interest to the eye after a character has exited, but the Incoming setting — it's new — holds interest, and can therefore be held for a (brief beats) time before a character enters. This is very reliable advice. Until you consider the context:

Joseph Steals Cocaine from a Telephone Booth scene from *Atlantic City*. After stealing the drugs, Joseph exits the phone booth — and the film frame. The shot holds on the empty phone booth for many beats. [*Figure 13.4*] The next cut immediately reveals a car pulling up to the curb. A drug dealer exits the car, and enters the phone booth to 'pick up' the cocaine.

Figure 13.4

Beats of Context

Ninety-nine percent of cuts might work exactly as Dmytryk advises. But, here the editor smartly granted greater preference to context than to reducing — what otherwise would be — unnecessarily prolonged beats. There was no wish to have the audience 'feel' that Joseph barely got away with the drugs. The 'hold' on the 'empty frame' represents an Emotional Time of some minutes.

The topic of our last chapter, the 180 Degree Rule: Harry Morant at the Preliminary Hearing scene in *Breaker Morant*. Profiles of Morant — in Close-Up — facing screen Right, and screen Left, are joined together. [*Figure 13.5*]

The context? A military hearing portrayed — by way of cuts — with rigid military pomp and posture.

Figure 13.5

A 180 Degree break? Absolutely!

I once overheard someone compare film editing to "solving a jigsaw puzzle." The fitting together of assorted pieces could permit a similarity; but pieces of fixed shape — requiring a one and only fit — are provided with a jigsaw puzzle. Film's contexts make the analogy unconvincing: A creative film editor can, and must, 'shape and reshape' the pieces to achieve an ideal fit.

conflicts in interest

"(There) are little things you do. The picture's been shot, you can't go back, but there are ways...."

— Harold Kress

Students seeking my help often declare that they are "too close to the material." I have come to believe that the opposite may be the case. The student is only close enough to think, but is not decisively close so as to feel. He cannot determine the essentials of Context — the integrity of the material.

It is one thing — and only one thing — to be 'feelingly' alert to the context of each and every cut; it is still surprisingly easy to lose the 'feel' of the story's particulars. More demanding is the context of a scene; still more the context of the sequence; and above all, the context of the entire film.

Good storytelling does not contradict information and impressions communicated to the audience. Editing requires an intimate, intense, and ongoing 'emotional reconsideration' of the audience's understandings, and attitudes, which are derived — in large part — by the editor's distribution (and re-ordering) of information.

TIP & HINT: Questions must be asked, and re-asked: What emotional impressions have prior scenes generated? Are associations to 'real world' experiences 'truthful?' Are established connections to story context(s) plausible? What understandings and feelings are being conveyed from scene(s) to sequence(s); and to the totality of the film's structure? Are these consistent where and when they have to be?

Editors need to be watchful of sudden appearances of conflicts in the interest of the story. Good editors pay (devoted) attention, and appreciate that — to paraphrase an adage about writers — there are no great editors... only great re-editors.

If you'll indulge me some conjecture, and 'educated' guessing, I'll 'show' you what I mean: Mother and Samuel in the Philadelphia Train Station scene, from *Witness*.

The Baltimore-bound train that mother and son were to 'catch' is delayed. As they walk to a station waiting area the boy spots a drinking fountain. He attempts to pull free of his mother's grip. She releases him, and as he explores the workings of the fountain, she takes a seat on a waiting area bench. The mother looks, and (almost) smiles at her son as he curiously plays with the newly 'discovered' machine. Samuel begins to walk from the fountain, and away from his mother. [*Figure 14.1*] We hear the mother's voice:

Figure 14.1

"Don't go far Samuel."

The boy turns and nods in agreement... [*Figure 14.2*]

Figure 14.2

...then continues his walk into the crowded station

During the boy's exploration of the wondrously immense space of the big city train station, he thinks he's spotted an Amish elder. [*Figure 14.3*] The boy happily approaches:

Figure 14.3

The man is an Hasidic Jew

Samuel moves off, soon coming upon a giant bronze statue high above the mezzanine of the station. [*Figure 14.4*]

Figure 14.4

The boy is enthralled

In a High Angle shot we see the mother 'find' him, [*Figure 14.5*] take his hand, and lead him...

Figure 14.5

...back to the waiting area

This sequence magnificently pulls off an exquisite ruse; a sleight of hand, more truly a 'sleight of eye,' in the interest of sustaining earlier — and fundamental — story (include character) impressions.

The mother and Samuel have left Lancaster County, Pennsylvania aboard an Amtrak train. This is Samuel's first trip, and perhaps the mom's as well. When we first see them in the crowded Philadelphia train station, we believe — and why wouldn't we — that the mother is on alert, very protective of Samuel. Yet she allows him to stroll away from her, into an unfamiliar place, crowded with dozens of strangers?

Let me speculate. At some point in the postproduction process, the director and/or the editor, heard a 'feelingly alert' warning 'clang!' Did they intend to show a careless, or negligent, mother? That is what they were 'suddenly' portraying. What are the consequences of this switch in manner? How will the audience now perceive the mother? Can anything be done to minimize the unwanted — and harshly disapproving — new impressions?

The editor could have cut from the boy at the drinking fountain to the later, and quiet, moment when mother and Samuel sit side by side on the waiting area bench, [*Figure 14.6*] deleting the scene of Samuel's wanderings, and its 'sorry' reflection on an Amish mother; and the (very likely) ire of the audience.

Figure 14.6

Samuel 'plays.' Cut to: Mother and Son on bench

It was decided (more of my guessing) that the scenes of the boy's exploration of the train station were worth keeping, perhaps even necessary for its structural beats prior to the Restroom Murder scene: the boy's sincere innocence before experiencing a brutal murder.

How did the editing avoid the audience's wrath at a 'negligent mother'? Why do I even suspect that a problem emerged?

I believe that the script called for Samuel to wander off, and the mother — busy with papers, and train tickets — to fail to notice. It seemed to me that the actions do run the risk of contradicting impressions, and 'real-life' associations presented earlier. The mother's 'sudden' lack of protective concerns in a hectic and unfamiliar setting made me wonder why so few people — there's me — 'feel' that the mother is carelessly inattentive to the safety of her son. With several screenings — and a little speculation — it is apparent that steps were taken in re-editing to avoid such a response by the audience, while keeping the naively adventurous Samuel off of the editing room floor.

When Samuel spots the drinking fountain, and attempts to pull free of his mother's hand he says, "Momma, look, look...." His mother responds — she clearly speaks to him — but her words have been deleted. Did the mother permit Samuel to 'have a look' at the fountain, but instruct him to stay within her sight?

Watch the seated mother: She examines travel instructions, telephone numbers, railway tickets from her purse; she looks at Samuel; [*Figure 14.7*] she is satisfied with his water fountain diversion.

Figure 14.7

Were these 'moments' originally reversed?

The next cut, back to Samuel, shows him ending his 'play' with the water; he begins to move away from the fountain, and away from his — she's still looking at him — mother. Samuel takes several steps, looking about as he moves off. Nearly six seconds elapse before we hear his mother's voice, "Don't go far Samuel." The boy turns, looks back, and nods — agreeing to the request. But, why does the mother allow Samuel to go so far before she cautions him? Indeed, why doesn't she call him back? Why don't we see the mother say, "Don't go far Samuel?"

What I think: The mother was never filmed saying, "Don't go far Samuel," because this was not scripted, nor the 'problem' realized in the screenplay. The line was recorded later, and used just before Samuel turns to the camera (the mother), and nods. Why is the mother's call to Samuel's walking away so late in coming? Because for the moment to work, the audience must see Samuel leave the drinking fountain, and see Samuel turn to acknowledge his mother's request. The Voice Over (Mother Off-Camera) has to be 'late' to 'be in sync' with Samuel's looking back, and nodding. If the original plan — and the shooting for it — had the mother distracted by the 'important' papers in her purse while Samuel wandered off, seen only by the audience — as I suspect — there would not be a shot of Samuel looking back in response to her request. Where did the editor get this shot?

Guessing a little more: The shot of Samuel (looking back) came from an outtake! Look at the boy's expression. His expression seems less likely to be a response to his mother, than to instructions from the director. The boy is being told, "Don't look around; just keep walking." Samuel is supposed to 'get away' while his mother is distracted.

That is why the boy's look-back is over his left shoulder. A planned look-back to the mother would call for the boy to turn to his right!

Another observation, which leads to my speculations: In the High Angle shot, in which the mother arrives to 'get' Samuel, and bring him back to the waiting area, we see Samuel turn to his mother before she gets to him. I'd guess that a line of dialogue was deleted here as well; a line that let Samuel know that his mother was approaching, but also made clear that the boy had slipped from the 'negligent' mother's sight!

I have squirreled away suppositions by the dozen; they 'play out' in my mind in various rhythms, and structures. I try to 'see' other possibilities, and enhancements.

In the spring of 1996 I worked on a portion of a feature film, *The Domain of the Senses*, produced by Europea de Cinema de Barcelona. The five parts, which made up the full film, were 'joined' in theme by the five senses. Sight, Hearing, Taste, and Smell were produced in Spain; Touch was shot and edited in New York City. The five short films were written and directed by five Spanish women. They avoided disputes over their 'assigned' senses: Evidently there was a director eager to take on Smell.

One of the directors was Nûria Olivé-Bellés, a dancer, choreographer, and former thesis student at the School of Visual Arts. While that is how I got the editing job, it is not the usual connection to find work. Most former students would prefer to stay clear of their ex-teachers: much better to begin a professional career fresh and free of all who knew you 'then.' In film production, that literally means 'with a clean slate.' Given the protocol, and hierarchy of a film's production it can be disagreeable to direct a former 'superior.' I accepted the editing offer because Nûria was an extraordinary filmmaker, always eager for genuine collaboration, and because Touch was to be cut on film. This appealed to me, because I suspected that with the ever-increasing influence of digital editing it might be my last chance to edit directly on film, and on the machine that I 'grew up with': the Moviola.

Touch was not to exceed 20 minutes. Nûria and I had planned to work from a first cut of approximately 45 minutes. We knew that there was a hurried schedule, but a cut of more than double the running time would allow us to uncover the story's needs. As it turned out, the producers wanted the work concluded with all due — and impossible — haste. From screening dailies, synchronizing picture and sound, getting the material coded and logged, pulling selected takes, and editing, we were given ten days to finish. We were scheduling backwards from the pre-arranged time the composer needed to complete the score. We did have a little room to maneuver: In an American film we would have had 90 feet per minute (35mm), but in Spain — and this was our measure — we were given 93.75 feet per minute, or 93 feet and 12 frames. While there are always 16 frames per foot in 35mm film, the difference in footage is derived from the 24 frames per second United States' film speed, and Spain's 25 frames per second.

I kept close 'watch' of the running time from my first cut. I kept footage counts as I edited each scene. The first assembly was 21 minutes and 23 seconds. I was close, and it would be easy to get down to 20 minutes, but what had we missed?

Nûria and I feared we might overlook all kinds of things. There seemed too little time to go beyond the 'think of it.' There was not enough time to be a good re-editor! We consoled each other by agreeing that we would accept whatever we 'missed' without burden of blame. I hoped that whatever I might 'miss' would not prove too dreadful. Would there be moments poorly constructed, or contexts disappointingly overlooked — unnoticed conflicts in interest?

Touch portrayed the relationship of a blind woman sculptor and her model. The sculptor used her hands to 'see' the model; later working in clay she would shape the 'memory' of her touch. On the last day — before a screening for the crew, and composer — I encountered a growing uneasiness. Confident in my 'feelings,' I screened, and re-screened, the finished work print. I could not find what it was that troubled me.

While walking to Penn Station, and during the train ride home, I 'played' scene after scene in my head...

Examples used in this chapter influenced my 'search': *Witness*, with its Train Station scene — you know my train ride reflections can be productive — and a masterfully resolved 'double-puzzle,' from *Rosemary's Baby*.

Rosemary and the Anagram scene: Rosemary's good friend Hutch has died. He has left her a book, *All Of Them Witches*, and a riddle: "The name is an anagram." Rosemary examines the book, and endeavors to find a solution with sixteen tiles from her Scrabble set. On her living room floor she spells out the book's title, and proceeds to arrange the tiles in new 'phrases.' [*Figure 14.8*] Rosemary attempts three arrangements, and 'calls it quits.'

Figure 14.8

More than an Anagram

The three arrangements result in:
1. Comes With The Fall
2. Elf Shot Lame Witch
3. How Is Hell Fact Me

The third uses fifteen letters... [*Figure 14.9*]

Figure 14.9

..."T" is left

Previous associations and unambiguous 'feelings' have led the audience to consider Hutch Rosemary's oldest, dearest, father-like friend. His 'deathbed' request that Rosemary be given the book, and riddle message, are passed along to Rosemary at Hutch's funeral. How can an audience believe that upon her arrival home from the cemetery, Rosemary undertakes but three tries to solve Hutch's riddle? What kind of lousy, disloyal, and — given the Contextual circumstances — reckless friend is this?

Her sad, yet sarcastic, "Now that really makes sense," and "Poor Hutch," [*Figure 14.10*] Rosemary's words — spoken aloud — as she gathers the tiles, won't 'forgive' her.

Figure 14.10

Rosemary calls it quits

The director, and editor were certainly on alert to this 'grave' contradiction in earlier impressions, and the likely consequence of the audience's weakening sympathy for Rosemary.

Before we 'discover' the (re)editing solution, let me point out one of the possible ways to side-step the problem: Delete the gathering of the Scrabble tiles — the Rosemary's about-to-quit beat — and cut from the three tries directly to Rosemary's realization — I trust you already know this, and that I won't ruin the film for you — that the anagram is not to be found in the name of the book, *All Of Them Witches*, but rather in the name of someone mentioned in the book. [*Figure 14.11*]

Figure 14.11

But! There is something to be said for keeping the Rosemary's about to quit beat — and it was decidedly kept — because of its engagingly dramatic beat in audience anticipation.

What is crucial is that in image — not in word — the audience accepts Rosemary's willingness to stop her search. Therefore, How Is Hell Fact Me, with the left over "T" was, in the re-editing, placed third and last. Rosemary is not getting closer — or 'warmer' — she is getting 'colder.'

But! How Is Hell Fact Me was not always in the third position. Elf Shot Lame Witch was scripted, shot, and originally edited as the third positioned 'solution.' How — in Hell — can we tell?

When Rosemary picks up the book, realizing the true 'source' of the anagram, and brings it to her, and the camera, [*Figure 14.12*] you can see, in the lower left corner of the screen:

Figure 14.12

The 'second solution' is still on the floor!

I have used this scene in class — and here — to point out the simple yet astounding power of image. Showing that Rosemary is 'unlikely' to solve the anagram eliminates — at least it 'softens' — conflicts in the story's previously presented, and persuasively developed, impressions of Rosemary's character; and (especially) her relationship to Hutch.

Ed Dmytryk, in his comments on Eisenstein's use of montage in *The Old and the New*, concludes that "(a) demonstration is always more convincing than a verbal argument."

Following a discussion about this scene a student brought to my attention that Elf Shot Lame Witch 'was still on the floor.' I now had another example of brilliant re-editing for all to 'see': to store with my other 'squirreled away' finds.

I drew a blank with Touch on my usually insightful train ride — I was alarmed by that. As I was about to fall asleep I understood what was 'troubling' me: The story had imperceptibly shifted. A hurried work schedule, and apprehension with the film's running time, had led me to overly refine and delete. The visual descriptions were 'suggesting' a relationship, not between artist and model, but chiropractor and patient. I couldn't wait to get back to the editing room to 'make repairs.'

I got to work at 8:00 a.m. and went through a reel of MOS (Mit Out Sound) Outtakes; and I found [*Figure 14.13*] what I needed:

Figure 14.13

The sculptor's hands…

…red with clay, rinsing in a small wooden water bucket. I positioned a selected portion of the shot at the beginning of a significant artist and model scene.

A minor 'touch' in very last-second re-editing, re-embodied the intended impressions.

stones
unturned

"The hardest thing to learn... is how to correct what's wrong without harming what's good."

— Dede Allen

Filmmakers who've attended film school are especially subject to overlook the larger view of context. This risk is most apparent when film school graduates take on a first feature, and most difficult to steer clear of when the director is also the screenwriter: The editing becomes an assembly of the precise (screenplay) pieces of the jigsaw. Perhaps it is that students become expert at making short films; and this easily lends itself to scene driven work.

TIP & HINT: The charm and excitement — immediate gratification — of a beloved shot can often 'win out' over obligations to a scene. The dramatic appeal and fascination of a scene can easily dominate storytelling's larger requirements. They are extremely difficult to resist.

Young filmmakers are frequently caught somewhere between movie buff and artist. This is marked by indiscriminate imitation of work that has won their affection, or through uncompromising — even militant — defense of their favorite director. Such hard-nosed allegiance might be admirable, but it precludes legitimate discussion about film.

There's a notion about (American) democracy that confuses "Everyone's entitled to an opinion" with the fact that some people's opinions are simply more relevant to a topic. I know, and respect this, each time I seek assistance from a film lab, optical house, or sound studio — I should add my doctor, dentist, and mechanic.

The retort, "That's your opinion!" not only goes without saying, it goes without thinking, and is, in effect, meaningless.

Most people go to the movies for an entertaining evening. Few people watch films with an interest in postproduction possibilities; and fewer inexorably take note of 'misses' — and 'near-misses' — occurring on screen.

I am one of the fewer. It is central to my continuous learning, ever-better teaching, and added value in my editing assignments.

I hope you've begun to 'see' more critically; and that I've helped to open a broader editing perspective. My observations are not about Right and Wrong, as much as a method of evaluation, workable choices, and improvement. So, if it will help me evade argument and wrath, I'll submit a sincere, "The following is (only) my opinion."

Three Scenes from *Fargo*:

Jerry Telephones His Father-In-Law scene
Jerry has arrived home to see that the 'deed is done.' The kidnappers have made off with his wife! Jerry, with grocery bags in each arm, stares into the bathroom. A cut shows a shower curtain rod lined with 'empty' rings. We hear Jerry's (Off-Camera) Voice Over:

> Yeah, Wade, it's Jerry.
> I don't know what to do.
> It's Jean...

Jerry has 'telephoned' his father-in-law to report Jean's kidnapping.

The Voice Over plays across another cut: A Close-Up of the shower curtain on the living room floor; a tilt of the camera into a Medium Shot, shows the 'snow-filled' TV screen [*Figure 15.1*] and broken glass from the shattered storm window.

Figure 15.1

Jerry's inflections feign anguish and panic

A cut to the kitchen reveals Jerry [*Figure 15.2*] at the telephone...

Figure 15.2

...But not on the telephone

Jerry is 'rehearsing' how to tell his father-in-law the 'bad' news.

This scene — actually three scenes shared — confuses the service of dramatic irony: The 'tension' in the images, and the audience's (possible) prying interest in Jerry's 'telephone presentation' is of false value — rambling affect — because the audience already knows that Jerry has ordered his wife's kidnapping. Given the previous distribution of information, the scene — with a concern for context — properly begins at the phone.

But! Can you imagine the cuts, and inflection variations, if the audience didn't know of Jerry's co-conspiratorial connection?

Carl and Gaear Arrive in Minneapolis scene
Carl explains the 'latest studies' concerning the risk of second-hand smoke, [*Figure 15.3*] before mentioning their imminent arrival into the city. Carl then proceeds with endless complaining about his partners 'quiet ways'; he's 'not spoken' during the entire ride.

Figure 15.3

The first time I screened *Fargo* it crossed my mind that an extra beat was needed between the Second-Hand Smoke Beat and the Here's Minneapolis Beat, to take us to the You Haven't Said a Word Beat, so that Carl's extended rant about Gaear's silence results from the 'effects' of the opening two beats.

In the end, this scene could have been effectively deleted: The next time we see the kidnappers they are at Jerry's house!

TIP & HINT: Connecting the beats will help to 'find' the rhythms that provide emotional subtext and motivate dialogue.

Consider as well — a gem of an unturned stone — that Carl was not bothered in the least by Gaear's smoking in the Jerry Meets the Kidnappers scene. [*Figure 15.4*] His concern then was, "You're late Jerry," and that his 'associate' has "peed three times."

Figure 15.4

Carl has no previous history of concern

Prior to their arrival in Minneapolis, Gaear smoked on the ride to Brainerd in the Carl and Gaear Discuss Stopping for Pancakes scene. [*Figure 15.5*] In neither of the earlier 'smoking scenes' did Carl signal that smoke disturbed him: no swipe of the smoky air, no opening of his window...

Figure 15.5

...No 'face' of displeasure

Such moments — and dialogue — occur when screenwriting and separate scenes are the 'driving force' of a film.

Raymond Chandler noted that he would have suffered less anguish in his career as a Hollywood screenwriter if he had realized all along that "screenwriting isn't even a second cousin to 'real' writing."

HINT: There are good reasons that, upon entering the theatre, moviegoers are not handed a feature screenplay. The house lights are not left 'burning.' Assembled ticket holders do not spend two hours reading.

Carl 'Battles' the Airport Parking Lot Toll Man scene
Carl has driven into the municipal parking lot at the airport. He is there to steal a license plate [*Figure 15.6*] for 'his' car.

Figure 15.6

Will Carl get away?

Upon exiting he seeks to avoid paying the parking fee by claiming he's decided not to park his car in the long-term lot "after all." The attendant makes clear that the fee must be paid, [*Figure 15.7*] and the scene escalates into Carl's harangue of insults.

Figure 15.7

What does this moment come out of?

The filmmakers again give priority to screenwriting — they could not pass up, by way of re-editing, their 'flair' for dialogue — rather than to the character(s) and story's plausibility; especially when you consider the context: Carl has kidnapped a woman; is driving a 'stolen' car; has killed two witnesses to the killing of a police officer; he has (just) stolen a license plate, and he 'stops' to battle a parking lot attendant to save four dollars.

Scene driven work often comes about when filmmakers forget their means of presentation: Abigail Tries to Seduce John scene, from *The Crucible*.

Imagine this scene as theatre: John and Abigail, alone on stage, in an abstract setting. Abigail's dialogue, with its tone — if not tumult — of anger, might not compel the audience to question Abigail's public spectacle, and sexual admissions. But, this is film.

The foundation of the problem is set when John Proctor leaves the Interior of Reverend Parris' house. John exits the frame in a Medium Shot; and another Medium Shot takes us to (Exterior) John nearing his horse. He looks back to see Abigail alongside a house. [*Figure 15.8*] This is not Reverend Parris' house, it is another, some distance away — we might remember this from Abigail's POV (Point Of View) shot from the second floor window of the Reverend's house as John arrived in Salem Village — but the exit and entrance beats from the Interior to the Exterior scene capture a 'feel' of real-time.

Figure 15.8

This is critical to the audience's 'setting' of the dialogue, and to reservations in presentation. The forceful theatrical performances disregard the 'realistic' Place and Time impressions that have brought us to the scene. John and Abigail are not alone on stage, but are 'in the company' of dozens of townsfolk in Salem.

HINT & TIP: Exit and Entrance beats can get you into a whole lot of Tick and Tock Trouble!

If the audience saw Abigail at the edge of the house, before John sees her, additional 'Time' would have been gained to assist in the 'separation' from Reverend Parris' house, and the proximity to the town fathers: a help of sorts.

John does 'look around' at times, demonstrating a concern with the 'delicacy' of the encounter. When he breaks free of Abigail's kiss, and her under-his-coat fondling, he makes his way back to the horse. Abigail pursues him, getting louder, and louder with verbal attack, which includes the 'confession' of an illicit affair. [*Figure 15.9*]

Figure 15.9

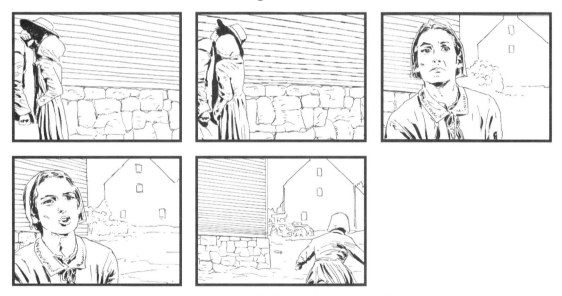

Can't anyone in Salem see or hear?

The Good Reverend could help: As discussed in the chapter on beats, Hale's arriving carriage could integrate the Abigail Tries to Seduce John scene and the John Greets Reverend Hale scene, and serve to 'soften' the purely theatrical construct of Exit (Abigail) and Entrance (Hale) Beats. If Abigail's Exit was a reaction to Reverend Hale's arrival — "Uh-oh! Someone's coming" — the beats would integrate; and a bit (beat) of 'real-world' experience could be returned to the scene: Abigail would 'bear witness' to the knowledge that sound does travel in Salem.

TIP & HINT: Editors should not be pleased too quickly.

reactions speak louder than words

"I touched wordless secrets that only the cinema can discover."

— Ingmar Bergman

When VHS tapes were first made available for screening on home VCRs, they were packaged to look like books. I suspect this was a marketing attempt to add prestige to an art form that sadly, first and foremost, is considered a smidgen of pop-culture. What other publicly presented art form is viewed while snacking on popcorn and Raisinettes, washed down with a bucket of cola-flavored ice?

The effort to attach 'distinction' to movies has shackled the art to literature and theatre. This is demonstrated — in abundance — with Voice Over Narration reading abridged versions of real or imagined novels and plays to the movie audience. In truth, this attests to the inability of many directors (and editors) to 'tell' a story through the juxtaposition of images — something film can do miraculously well, and something no other 'storytelling' form enjoys.

Words — especially in great number — cause discord between the senses. The eyes can so easily 'understand' vast quantities of references, and atmosphere. This might be the reason we shut our eyes to identify a taste, or a smell; we shut our eyes when we are touched, or kiss; and concerted listening persuades our eyes to close. Cinema should not try to be theatre or radio.

Eisenstein's August 1928 Statement — jointly signed by V.I. Pudovkin and G.V. Alexandrov — describing the authors' misgivings about the 'new' invention is remarkably prophetic. To use sound "for highly cultured dramas and other photographed performances of a theatrical sort... will destroy the culture of montage.... Only a contrapuntal use of sound in relation to the visual montage piece will afford a new potentiality...."

Film is a legitimate art form, but its potential is frequently diverted by the human voice. Raymond Chandler insisted that the best scene he ever wrote consisted of three lines of dialogue, spoken by the same actress, "Uh-huh. Uh-huh. Uh-huh." He explained that this was not the initial writing.

Screen the opening scenes from *The Lover*. I know of no film that equals its damaging use of Voice-Over Narration.

In their effort to present a 'prestigious novel,' the filmmakers begin with 'pretty' Close-Ups of a pen to paper. An abridged and altered version of author Marguerite Duras' opening pages begins: A Voice Over 'reads' to the audience. The voice is that of an elderly — hard-smoking — woman 'telling' us about her early adolescence. What we are watching is not (now) occurring... it has happened long ago. There is a price to pay for this, and it is exorbitant! Immediacy, urgency, and engaging enchantment are taken from the audience.

A 'literary form' lures the filmmakers into a structure that is unnecessarily complicated — starting, and re-starting, the story several times. The damage done to beautifully elegant footage arises in the show and tell 'staging,' and its near-silly redundancies. [*Figure 16.1*]

Figure 16.1

"*I am taking the ferry that crosses... Crossing a branch of the Mekong... The ferry crossing of the Mekong... I wear lamé shoes... I wear a man's hat...*"

In contrast with no Voice Over, and with a (very) modest amount of dialogue — as in the Girl and Business Man Drive to Saigon in a Chauffeured Limousine scene [*Figure 16.2*] from *The Lover* — the storyshowing is superb, and we are under the spell of images.

Figure 16.2

Authentic storyshowing

Voiceover Narration (nearly) disables the drama of an entire Sequence in The Joy Luck Club. [*Figure 16.3*] Beginning with the Husband Arrives at the Baby's Birthday Celebration With His Mistress scene, it 'runs' through the Mother Bathes the Baby scene.

Figure 16.3

Showing in Pictures; Telling in Subtitles and Voice Over: Show and Tell and Tell

The Voice Over 'explains' the psychologically vengeful reasoning behind the mother's terrible deed... before the act! Screen the Mother Bathes the Baby scene with the audio on mute. Even with the loss of the bath water's drip-drip, the scene is simple; it is (near) perfection!

HINT: Without the voiceover 'telling,' the scene becomes a wonderful example of the paradoxical bond between Thinking and Feeling!

Dra·ma: noun. A series of events involving conflicting forces.

TIP & HINT: The 'process' of storytelling should not be the 'force' in conflict.

Can there ever be voiceover narration that works; that does augment storyshowing? According to Chapter 13 there must be!

In the thesis film *Life Before Me*, the young man — his name is Wilson — falls from the roof. [*Figure 16.4*] On his way down — in Voiceover Narration — he begins 'telling' his story...

Figure 16.4

"I couldn't believe I actually fell off. I simply lost my balance and now I was falling. I just couldn't believe it.
And, in a weird way, I can't remember ever thinking so clearly..."

The Context in *Life Before Me* provides a numinous opportunity for the voice over. The story is presented in flashbacks that, at times, return the audience to the 'still' falling Wilson. Seeing as no one can fall from the roof of a city building, and live to tell us his story, Wilson's voice over — an absolute impossibility in real life — is movie magic that 'pulls in' the audience. A worthy 'fix' was also accomplished: All of the voice over was dropped back — from a little to a lot — so that it would come after the audience could take pleasure, and information, from the images.

Consider film's more customary use of the human voice: Dialogue.

There are bits and pieces [of dialogue] that require deletion: Words, lines, phrases, or passages appear in the screenplay to serve as — what might be deemed — Convincing Material; or as cues for reading clarity, and actor inflection.

Convincing material helps the screenwriter 'create' the veritability of characters — to convince the writer, and reader — on paper: The 'scripted people' do exist! Convincing material often survives into the dailies, and 'appears' in two forms:
    1. Profuse use of First Names.
    2. Extensive Personal Exposition.
In 'real life' people seldom address each other by name while they speak, especially when there are only two people. In film, people (nearly) never utter a line

without including the other character's first name. You can delete most of them...
perhaps all!

For a good example — it goes without Showing — of 'name calling' that went
from script to dailies to finished film, watch Dr. Frank and His Brother Harlan —
Harlan, That's Harlan — in a Bar scene from *Novocaine*. The film also contains
unnecessary and 'wounding' Voiceover Narration.

Convincing material 'heard' as personal exposition exists as (long) passages in
which a character 'tells' us about personal history, or experience. We do not
need to know a character's place (and time) of birth, nor which kindergarten he
attended, in order to believe he is 'real.'

TIP: Most especially, it's a good idea to delete (or greatly reduce) exposition of personal experience that the audience would rather be seeing than hearing; or, that
has little (or nothing) to do with the immediate needs of the story.

Examples of the above can be found throughout *The Spitfire Grill*.

Cues depict a character's impressions or emotions. They are often followed by a
phrase that works better without the cue:

CUE	PHRASE
"I'm getting nervous.	We should have heard from him by now!"

Delete the Cue. Keep the Phrase.

Cues usually take an audience 'out' of emotional engagement with the moment;
they are a form of detrimental tell and tell.

Historian Henry Adams described Thomas Jefferson's intelligence as "intellectual sensuousness." Good dialogue editing — good editing of all material — creates a kind of Cognitive Emotion in the audience. It brightly links Thinking and
Feeling: Thinking becomes an authentic sixth sense. This seeming contradiction
to chapter 13 is not.

HINT: Mother Bathes the Baby scene, from The Joy Luck Club, without its Voice
Over!

An entire audience's Sensual Thinking will — astonishingly — 'Match-Up': "She
wouldn't hurt the baby. No! She's not going to hurt the baby..."

In a 'test' I initiated in an Introduction to Film course, I played two scenes for students over a three-year period. Discussions, after each of the screenings, verified identical Thinking and Feeling, or cognitive emotions, in the students:

1. The Rape scene from *The Virgin Spring*.
Karin is stopped as she tries to leave the 'picnic.' She is attacked and raped. Crying in gasps and squeaking sobs, she moves away [*Figure 16.5*] from her attackers. The 'mute' brother clubs her across the head.

Figure 16.5

During the interval between the rape and murder every student terrifyingly reflected: "At least they didn't kill her."

2. The Bus Accident scene from *The Sweet Hereafter*.
The school bus skids off the road. It crashes the guard rail; rolls down an embankment, and still upright, onto a frozen river. [*Figure 16.6*] The ice begins to break; the bus disappears.

Figure 16.6

During the interval between the school bus' slide onto the frozen river, and its sinking below the ice, every student shockingly reflected: "At least the bus hasn't rolled over."

In "Cutting Emotional Attachments" I mentioned the paradox created by the number of cuts passing before the eyes of the audience. The intercutting concept promoted in that chapter relates an association between 'finding' emotion in the editing and the inconspicuousness of the cuts. Just as a single appearance of MOS (Mit Out Sound) Shots makes for obviousness — remember Someone's Going Through the Dresser scene? — dialogue, which is played consistently on the speaker, will do the same. The eye and ear will be 'hit' at every cut point; each edit symmetrically 'marked' for the audience. This happens because of the (more or less) parallel structure of image to dialogue and — most important — because its 'talking' snippets are unlikely to craft conversation — actual dialogue — or 'find' emotion.

The intercutting paradox is at its best when reactions are the guiding weight in dialogue editing. Reactions also keep us within the good effects of thinking and feeling.

In the dailies, dialogue is often closer to monologue. The actors' readings might be credible, even vigorous, but incomplete in 'sought-after' rhythms. For one thing, actors know their lines and the lines of the other actors — at least the last three words — and usually follow each other's lines (too) quickly.

TIP: You'll be surprised how often this is discernible in the dailies: Actors will transfer their gaze to another actor before that actor has begun to speak, anticipating whose turn is next.

HINT: Film acting is not — nor does it require — an impeccable continuum as it (usually) is in theatre.

In many ways the dailies represent a (cinematographic and audio) final dress rehearsal — a trial run. The editor (and director) must then orchestrate, and 'conduct' the dailies into an inclusively accomplished performance: Pacing — beats and rhythms — transposition of lines, and deletions.

The essential performance is more easily discovered in the Close-Ups: Master Shots can too easily 'hide,' or 'misrepresent,' what is vital to the scene, and performance. It is in the Close-Ups that the editor — later the audience — can see the varied, changing, and most subtle expressions in the eyes, lips, and posture of the actor's face. This allows the editor to 'see' that words can beneficially be deleted, while up on the screen their consequence and 'meaning' will be unmistakable.

The attentiveness to reactions is the key to unlocking mere monologue, to permit the dialogue to bring about spontaneous, and believable, character to character contact.

A Lost Truck Driver Recognizes Colonel Kotov from *Burnt By the Sun*.

The driver approaches the car carrying the uniformed Colonel. [*Figure 16.7*] In editing, several beats were 'added' following the driver's obvious recognition of Kotov — his mouth drops wide open — but, before he can ask if it is Colonel Kotov, a reaction on the Colonel expresses his pleasure at being recognized — he laughs in delight!

Figure 16.7

We 'feel' the contact!

Frequently there is a need for a Double Reaction: Frank and the Patrolman of the Month Get a Free Lunch scene from *Serpico*. Frank naively asks for something other than the 'Special Of The Day.' We know that he shouldn't have requested "a roast beef on roll," [*Figure 16.8*] because...

Figure 16.8

... of a perfectly timed Double Reaction on Charley; and he is offended!

An inventive 'discovery' of a needed reaction can be found in the Frau Mozart Seeks the Aid of Salieri scene from *Amadeus*. The last of Frau Mozart's three reactions to Salieri's 'demands' is a 're-use' of an earlier beat. [*Figure 16.9*] Objecting to Frau Mozart's addressing him as "Your excellency," Salieri 'scolds' her; assures her of his accessibility; and then identifies himself as a 'commoner,' "Just like your husband." Frau Mozart reacts to each; her third 'comes' from the On-Camera — over Salieri's left shoulder — shot of an earlier reaction to the 'delectability' of the Capezzoli di Venere (Nipples Of Venus) treat.

Figure 16.9

"Mmmmm" is deliciously smart

At the School of Visual Arts we use a scene from *Law and Order* in our editing classes. (We have gone from cutting the exercise on film to 'cutting' on a computer.)

INTERIOR. INTERROGATION ROOM. DAY. [*Figure 16.10*]
Detective Van Buren is interrogating Julia — a young woman claiming to be the victim of a sexual assault.

Figure 16.10

A Close-Up of Each

JULIA
He grabbed me, stuck his tongue down
my throat.

VAN BUREN
You try to push him away?

JULIA
I tried but he's bigger than me.

VAN BUREN
All right. After the tongue what
happened?

JULIA
Do I have to do this?

VAN BUREN
He didn't commit a Class "A" felony
with his tongue Julia....

On paper, the dialogue 'makes perfect sense'; at the least it doesn't 'appear' overly problematic! During the editing, the actors' 'expressions' can be effectively — emotionally — read, and therefore 'played' and attuned. Delete Julia's last line, "Do I have to do this?" and a powerful beat — spontaneous contact — is created: the result of her embarrassment, and the 'painful' questioning. Van

Buren's last line becomes far more intense, and brings eloquent ambivalence to the audience. They are uncomfortable to 'eavesdrop,' but nonetheless eager to hear all the details.

Production procedures provide dailies with repeated lines of dialogue through each of the camera set-ups: There is 'identical' dialogue with each Image.

TIP: Here is an oh-so-simple technique to 'find' Performance.

Begin by quickly assembling — in checkerboard fashion — one Close-Up of each character. The first 'clip' contains the opening line(s) of dialogue. From then on each and every cut should begin with a character listening (reacting) to the second reading of the very same line — or lines — of dialogue. This second reading is the Off-Camera Dialogue.

Without a single frame of Picture or Sound left out — except Slates — this produces:

JULIA (on Camera): In Sync Dialogue: He grabbed me, stuck his tongue down my throat.

Cut To:

VAN BUREN (on Camera): {OC dialogue} – He grabbed me, stuck his tongue down my throat. In Sync Dialogue: You try to push him away?

Cut To:

JULIA (on Camera): {OC dialogue} – You try to push him away? In Sync Dialogue: I tried but he's bigger than me.

Cut To:

VAN BUREN (on Camera): {OC dialogue} – I tried but he's bigger than me. In Sync Dialogue: All right. After the tongue what happened?

Cut To:

JULIA (on Camera): {OC dialogue} – All right. After the tongue what happened? In Sync Dialogue: Do I have to do this?

Cut To:

VAN BUREN (on Camera): {OC dialogue} – Do I have to do this?
In Sync Dialogue: He didn't commit a Class "A" felony with his tongue, Julia....

Screen (and listen) to the assembly with the doubled lines. This allows for discoveries of deletions in either (or both) dialogue or image; discoveries of advantageous redundancies — you're hearing the lines twice — and for discoveries of critically needed pauses in Sound, and reactions in Picture — especially when inflections (or topics) change.

HINT: Editors can be too quick to remove redundancies. Be careful! There are some very good ones.

Van Buren's next to last line begins with "All right." What if you create an expanded pause — beat — before and after it? Won't that intensify the apprehension in Julia? The audience?

For a remarkably speedy way to discover how reactions work to link thinking and feeling, eliminate the second, or Off-Camera, dialogue — in the audio only — which will leave (long) pauses on each incoming cut of picture: Each character 'contemplates' what has been said by the other. You'll be able to tell where 'anticipation' might be more effective: an interruption in words, or expression(s), in the face — or body.

TIP: You will find that about 30% of the cuts in this simple system will get you surprisingly close to the needed rhythms, provide a quick and credible edit, and — most fundamental and cheerful of all — let you feel the requirements of the scene.

HINT: You might find a need for a 'better' take: Nothing reveals the 'best' take quicker than an assembly, because it furnishes (an early) context! You'll be able to 'see' where a Master Shot is 'called for.' You'll 'learn' that it's far easier to tell if, where, and why a Master Shot is needed by starting with Close-Ups, than if you work the other way around.

Dede Allen — interviewed by Vincent LoBrutto for his book, *Selected Takes: Editors On Editing* — recalled the 'official' advice from her early days at Columbia Pictures: "Now young lady... you always cut from a master to a closer shot." Her (now) experienced response: "Well, that's bullshit." Ms. Allen goes on to suggest another — more than likely — outcome to a scene, "You sometimes start with a close-up."

TIP & HINT: I am not pronouncing a solution to every 'end product.' I am suggesting you get started by working from Close-Ups. It is simply a practical method for getting to the "feel of it."

TIP & HINT: You can also 'work' MOS (Mit Out Sound) shots — or combinations of Synchronized and MOS shots — with this doubling. Double the actions: Entrances, Exits, and Movements within the scene. It makes for a beat-ready, subtext-ready, and context-ready assemblage.

An example of this practical approach to starting, but a poor choice in finishing: The Sheriff Arrives at the Bus Depot scene(s) from *The Trip to Bountiful*. [*Figure 16.11*]

INTERIOR. CAR. NIGHT.
and
INTERIOR. BUS DEPOT. NIGHT.

Figure 16.11

Joined in confusion

The final edit maintains the rough cut's two openings:
1. A car (Sheriff) drives up to the bus depot. The car is turned off, and the driver exits the car.
2. A cat sits in front of the (Interior) bus depot door. The 'someone' from the car (Sheriff) enters, and picks up the cat.

The 'join' only makes sense in an early assembly: An approach that later 'shows' choices via possible combinations of the two shots — or a deletion of one.

The two shots easily integrate so as to prevent a start and stop and start. That is, if the Sheriff's arrival is shown in the Interior Car scene, a cut to the cat in the Interior Bus Depot scene could occur sooner. No need for the car to turn off, or the driver to exit in the 'Exterior' Shot. The sounds — engine turn-off; door open, and close — could 'play' over the shot of the cat, which could 'play' through the Sheriff's entrance.

The Exterior, INTERIOR CAR scene (Image) could be deleted altogether, and the Sound alone utilized.

HINT: The Sheriff picking up the cat — Physical Life — after he enters the bus depot — Physical Action — is a fine touch. Having the Sheriff toss the cat onto the sleeping Clerk is a Stone Unturned. [*Figure 16.12*] Why would the Sheriff do such a thing — given the information the Sheriff possesses — finding Mrs. Watts asleep on the bus depot bench?

Figure 16.12

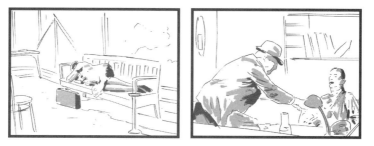

It would help to delete the cat's shriek

Preserving Reactions — rather than the On-Camera speaker — as the decisive influence in a Dialogue scene, requires an integration of four aspects:

1. Contemplation: The audience 'reads' (thinks and feels) a character's expression(s).
2. Anticipation: The audience 'understands' that a character is 'getting the idea.'
3. Observation: The audience sees the place and the spatial relationship(s) of the characters within the scene setting.
4. Participation: The audience is instantaneously 'in the scene.'

HINT: The four (often) rely upon the eyes of the characters: an indication that a character(s) is 'getting the attention' of another character(s). Remember the 'Popeye' Doyle and Russo 'Rough-Up' a Suspect scene in *The French Connection*?

TIP: You can use the Double the Dialogue/Checkerboard System when there are more than two characters: Use a cut of each listening (reacting) to the repeated — Off Camera — line(s), cutting last to the next character to speak. Then, repeat the cycle.

A scene which vividly expresses this: Morant, Whitten, and Hancock Meet Major Thomas scene from *Breaker Morant*.

A Master Shot is used sparingly [*Figure 16.13*] to 'situate' the soldiers throughout the scene. Its positioning in the scene might have been the last decided upon.

Figure 16.13

Whitten sits; Major Thomas sits

The dialogue — in Close-Ups — overlaps reactions with such precise integrity, that the cuts evaporate into the breadth of performance. So much so, that the audience would be hard pressed to recall which of the characters was featured on screen when (specific) lines of dialogue were heard.

HINT: A sizeable portion of this scene demonstrates the ease of the doubling dialogue technique — when there are more than two characters — to assist in discovering the 'right' performance. [*Figure 16.14*]

Figure 16.14

ˆ**Reactions carry the weight...**

...distributing information, creating surefire conversation — genuine dialogue — and (emotional) subtext.

Colin and Friend Mock the Minister scene from *The Loneliness of the Long Distance Runner*: a scene of exquisite cinema! Reaction/Images 'minus' audio. [*Figure 16.15*] Colin turns off the sound on the "telly" while they view the 'talking head' government minister's address to the nation. They mock the minister's gestures, 'breaking into' out-of-control laughter.

Figure 16.15

Such simple 'expression' in no other Medium

ask
gertrude
stein

"The magicians who bottle the genie are the actors. The magician who lets the genie out of the bottle is the editor."

— Rob Nilsson

An actor will endeavor to 'grasp' a scene by probing the objective(s) of the character he is portraying. Editors will find it helpful to ask, "What is the scene about?" and consider the question(s) every scene proposes: What information is revealed? How is it revealed?

HINT: In the end these questions get the editor to the discovery of sequence(s).

The last question: Does the scene include the asking of questions?

Questions can dictate the rhythms — subtext — of a scene; allow well 'disguised' exposition; and assist in constructing sequences. How far from the question is the answer?

Questions about questions include: Are answers happily given? Are they given at all? What answers are best deleted?

If a scene concludes with a question, it is usually best to leave the answer for (sometime) later; and it is better than best if the answer is depicted rather than told!

Deleting an answer to a scene-concluding question, easily and dramatically, fulfills David Mamet's proposition that the audience must want an answer to "What's going to happen next?"

Scene-concluding questions:

Frau Mozart Seeks the Aid of Salieri from *Amadeus*.
Mozart's wife has brought her husband's manuscripts. She asks Salieri for his help in obtaining a court position for Mozart. Salieri 'listens' to the music in his mind's ear. He is overwhelmed by Mozart's genius. [*Figure 17.1*]

FRAU MOZART
Then you'll help us?

Figure 17.1

Salieri does not answer

Serpico Questions the Prisoner from *Serpico*.
Serpico tries to win the trust of the suspect; he takes off the handcuffs and gets him coffee. He asks him to divulge the whereabouts of his cohorts. [*Figure 17.2*]

FRANK SERPICO
You talk to me. Save yourself.

Figure 17.2

The prisoner does not answer

Galvin Confronts the Admitting Nurse from *The Verdict*.
After an all night effort to find a 'missing' nurse — a nurse crucial to a civil trial in Boston — Galvin goes to New York City to convince the nurse to 'return' and testify. [*Figure 17.3*]

GALVIN
Will you help me?

Figure 17.3

The nurse does not answer

Awaiting an answer while 'resting' on a reaction shot prompts the thinking/feeling response in the audience: "Oh my! I wonder if he'll tell." "I hope he doesn't." "I wish she'd help." It is the simplest of good storytelling — storyshowing — strategies.

Several of the films in this chapter employ a trial — an examination before a judicial panel. This might give a helpful tip & hint to the editor — and actor. Here is an allegory: To examine through questions, the 'trials and tribulations' of the character(s) — as in subjected to suffering, grief, sorrow, or hardship. Why would an audience want to meet the character(s) at this time? What and where are the obstacles confronting the character(s)? And! By way of twists and turns, "What is going to happen next?"

Pascali's Island is a near-classic example of this kind of 'arrangement.' Basil himself says, "Not some kind; the best kind!"

I ask the reader a question: What do you get with an answer? Do you really want an answer?

It is rumored that when Gertrude Stein lay dying, her companion Alice B. Toklas beseeched, "Gertrude! What is the answer?" Gertrude slowly turned toward Alice answering, "Alice! What is the question?"

Ben is Fired from *Leaving Las Vegas*.
Ben sits in Bill's Office. He is holding his final paycheck.

BILL
Have you thought about what you'll do now? [Figure 17.4]

Figure 17.4

BEN: I was thinking I'd move out to Las Vegas

The proceeding scenes have lost their engaging energy. We know Ben's plan; and in the end, the (follow-up) sequence demonstrates little more than that Ben wasn't lying to Bill — and the audience.

Reverend Hale Demands an Answer from *The Crucible*.
Reverend Hale asks the assembled girls to tell him who it was that led them to dance around the fire. One of the girls points to Abigail. Abigail denies responsibility.

REVEREND HALE
Tell me who that was. Who? [Figure 17.5]

Figure 17.5

ABIGAIL: Tituba!

The next scene begins with the Town Fathers ordering Tituba from her shelter. [*Figure 17.6*]

Figure 17.6

"Snitching" on Tituba — answering the question — as an end to the previous scene brings up possibilities worth mentioning.

Ending with the "snitch" might generate greater emotion if the audience then sees Tituba going about her daily chores before the arrival of the Town Fathers. Tituba does not know what the audience knows: The 'authorities' will be coming for her! A delay in the Town Fathers Grab Tituba scene might also be of structural service. Had the "snitching" answer been deleted (with or without an extra beat or two), the audience's thinking/feeling response would have been significantly advanced: "Oh no! Abigail has told!!" Or perhaps: "Good! Abigail has saved herself!!!"

What if no question ended the *Leaving Las Vegas* and *The Crucible* scenes? Think/Feel about that as an answer!

TIP & HINT: Consider Context.

Morant, Whitten, and Hancock Meet Major Thomas from *Breaker Morant*. The scene's last lines are in answer to:

WHITTEN
Do you think they're going to imprison us or cashier us?
My father, if he found out....

MAJOR THOMAS (interrupting)
They told you! There's several murder charges. The penalty's death!

Major Thomas' interrupting phrase, "They told you!" is played with an unusual break (beat) — a postproduction discovery — before his next phrase: A long pause across reactions on Morant and Hancock. The audience is about to get information — "the penalty's death" — that was already given to, or should have been 'clear' to the soldiers. Following Whitten's reaction of the Major's last phrase there is a reaction on Morant, and another reaction on Whitten. Thomas' 'answer' is not precisely a response to the two possibilities in Whitten's question; it establishes a 'mortal' apprehension throughout the story.

A last reaction on Whitten ends the scene — it reveals 'an end' to his naiveté.

Much of the dialogue in the scene is constructed with questions. The most decisive directed to Major Thomas. Take note of the pauses — beats — before he answers two important questions:

MORANT
1. As a matter of interest, how many Courts Martial have you done?

WHITTEN
2. But you have handled a lot of court cases back home sir...?

The answer to both questions? [Figure 17.7]

Figure 17.7

MAJOR THOMAS: "None"

I think it fair to deduce that the beats which precede "None" span more time in the edited form than in the dailies. Major Thomas' answer to Morant is heard on a reaction shot of Morant — 'opening' enough beats to permit a 'double' asking of the question. Major Thomas then takes many additional beats — with the good help of the editor — to turn his head, and eyes (to pay attention), toward Whitten to answer his question. This time Major Thomas is On-Camera. Why 'delay' the answer(s)?

Because Major Thomas does not "happily answer"!

TIP & HINT: A very happily answered question might call for an — anticipatory — interruption. The answerer 'can't wait' to respond to the questioner. Answering beats and rhythms can help establish subtext.

Joe and Mary (in a Diner) Question What Went Wrong With Their Marriage scene from *Midnight Family Dinner*, a thesis student's (very) dark comedy. [*Figure 17.8*]

Two New York City cops 'bust' a prostitute and her ten-year-old son — who is (also) her pimp. As it turns out, the male cop is the ex-husband of the prostitute, and the father of the ten-year-old. Shortly before the birth of his child, he 'skipped' town, abandoning his pregnant wife during a severe New York winter.

Figure 17.8

A Diner Dinner Answer

Midnight Family Dinner
Director/Editor, Akira Shimokawa

MARY
... You really screwed us up... all of us... our whole family!
And where did you go after you left?

JOE
Florida for a couple of years....

Mary's opening phrase is delivered with attacking animosity. "And where did you go after you left?" is asked with doubt, and insecurity. It was a difficult task for the actress to 'shift inflection.' In each of her Close-Ups, the actress' eyes revealed that she didn't remember the second phrase. Then, though her eyes confirmed recollection, the actress looked down — she had to take pause — to 'gather herself' for the inflection change.

It goes without saying that it is unacceptable to let the audience 'see' that an actor has forgotten her lines. In film the editor can provide an assist — an actor in theatre will always be vulnerable.

The actress created a beat by looking down, but it was an obvious component of the performance process — not 'in character.' The 'look down' had to be deleted. Another beat was needed between phrases: a reaction of Joe? Or two beats? What if the 'new inflected phrase' is heard before we see a Close-Up of Mary, after the actress has looked up?

In all of Joe's Close-Ups (in the dailies), the actor answered Mary's question in 2.5 seconds.

HINT: Actors know each other's lines!

Then, in the last take of the last set-up (a short establishing shot meant 'only' to be used for a reaction on a character at the diner's counter) [*Figure 17.9*] the actor 'caught' the rhythm. Joe took 7.5 seconds. Joe was not happily answering Mary's question, and...

Figure 17.9

...it worked!

The actor's 'discovered' rhythm — and the correct subtext — was now the editor's responsibility: Make the question and answer work in the Close-Ups.

TIP: Editors! Keep Gertrude Stein in mind.

tipping
the
scales

"For me the creative process is more one
of discovery than creation."

— James Lee Burke

During the summer of 2002, French anthropologist Michel Brunet introduced the world to Toumai (Goran for "hope of life"), a fossil skull found in Central Africa, belonging to our earliest known hominid ancestor. The discovery of *Sahelanthropus tchadensis* is evidence that our link to chimpanzees is (for now) some 2-4 million years earlier than previously estimated. Isn't this further proof that The Eye Is Quicker? I'd say the eye now 'looks' much, much quicker! The discovery calls to mind Walter Murch's analogy of chimpanzees and editors. Don't laugh! Murch isn't poking fun at editors — or at chimps for that matter.

Murch points out that humans share nearly identical DNA with chimpanzees, yet are (apparently) distinguishable. His analogy suggests a correlation between chimp and human DNA, and identical (uncut) dailies in the hands of different editors. The ever-so-slight difference in the genetic code in the DNA that makes a chimp a chimp, and a human, human, clearly makes all the difference in appearance; as would the 'code' — arrangements of the film footage — assembled by different editors from identical dailies. Might the differences in the editor's arrangements reveal identifiable 'codes'?

The distinctions are linked to the nine key elements. They may well be considered nine key 'codes':

1. Story
2. Place
3. Character
4. Physical Action
5. Physical Life
6. Dialogue
7. Information first known to audience
8. Information first known to character
9. Information learned by audience and character simultaneously

I know that my former Continuing Ed student from Germany — and perhaps Einstein himself — would urge that my second 'code' be Time/Space. This chapter is not theoretical. I use "Place" in its most practical application — not pertaining to any law of physics — to mean locations of scenes.

The arrangement(s) of these 'codes' is of utmost significance: It separates second-rate from inspired editing.

With Context in mind (at all times), inspired editing will be discovered in the balance of the nine 'codes.'

Balance: An instrument for determining weight; comparison as to weight amount, importance; composition or placement of elements; a state of equilibrium or equipoise.

The definition's reference to "composition or placement of elements" is familiar in two-dimensional design concepts, as in 'Formal Balance.' Formal balance is easily appealing. It instantly — often misleadingly — embraces order and control. Formal balance in film editing can easily miss the breadth of a scene; and in the end, it is the leading contributor to 'playing' a filmed synopsis, rather than a presentation 'in full.'

For the film editor, the balance of the nine 'codes' is exceptionally effective when 'Informal': Asymmetrical! Successful asymmetry requires an integration of the nine 'codes.'

Let's go back to the *Law and Order* editing exercise. In Julia's Close-Up, Van Buren delivers her last line after leaning forward — and toward Julia. [*Figure 18.1*] We are behind Van Buren and over her right shoulder. The camera 'moves in' with her.

Figure 18.1

"He didn't commit a class 'A' felony with his tongue..."

Julia's eyes shift to Van Buren. Van Buren's lean precedes her dialogue; and as it happens, the camera has come to rest, and Julia has shifted her eyes. At first glance and listen, the shot looks unusable — it 'feels' clumsy, out of sorts; it might even be deemed 'Out Of Sync.' The dialogue and physical action — Van Buren's lean — 'codes' are separated, and conspicuous in their 'production arranged' combination.

Shift the audio: We are behind Van Buren; we do not see her mouth: There is no concern for lip synchronization.

HINT: We'll see how often being 'In Sync' can be 'Out of Sync.'

By advancing the audio so that Van Buren's dialogue is heard just before Julia shifts her eyes, and before Van Buren, and the camera, have finished their moves, the shot is 'fixed.' We have integrated Van Buren's dialogue and the physical action.

HINT: Julia's 'shifting eyes' following the start of Van Buren's dialogue works — getting Julia's attention — the same way as the 'mismatches' in *The French Connection* scene: 'Shifting eyes' proceed from dialogue.

Asymmetry can be established by a rearrangement of beats: 'Formal' scene Openings and Closings — entrances and exits — might 'feel' tidy, and logical, but they can easily yield sagging-dragging moments.

In *Breaker Morant*, a postproduction solution creates an asymmetrical entrance — an integration of 'codes' and beats.

Morant, Whitten, and Hancock Await the Findings of the Court Martial scene.

Peter Hancock stands atop a table to recite a limerick; he 'kicks-up' a fuss, striking items on the table. At that moment Major Thomas and another officer enter, [*Figure 18.2*] not noticed by the three soldiers. Hancock delivers his limerick…

Figure 18.2

…Only then do the three soldiers become aware of the 'entrants'

HINT: The entrance of Major Thomas forms a combination in beats: The Limerick Recitation beat [Physical Action/Dialogue] is integrated with the Entrance [Physical Action] beat. This discloses a crucial distinction to theatre. Theatre 'obliges' each beat to be separated and completed: The Limerick Recitation beat would conclude before the Entrance beat.

HINT & TIP: The means of presentation is steadfastly linked to Context.

The integration of beats — the nine 'codes' are a support in 'spotting' them — is vital to an understanding of Editing Asymmetry.

Frau Mozart Seeks the Aid of Salieri scene from *Amadeus*.
Salieri stands and moves from the table: Physical Action. He holds and reads Mozart's manuscripts: Physical Life. A new beat is initiated: Salieri 'listens' to Mozart's music in his mind's ear. A cut takes us back to an earlier beat: Frau Mozart enjoys (another) tasty pastry treat: Physical Life, before proceeding with the new beat. [*Figure 18.3*]

Figure 18.3

AND! We see what Salieri doesn't. We hear what Frau Mozart doesn't

Robbers and Hostages in the Bus scene from *Dog Day Afternoon.*
Sonny excitedly proclaims the success of their 'escape,' "We did it Sal..." Several
new beats are played — the release of one hostage; an FBI agent's directive —
before there is a return [*Figure 18.4*] to the Excited Sonny beat: Dialogue.

Figure 18.4

The editor did it!

In each scene the editor has crafted Asymmetry by way of integrating beats of
(the) key 'codes.'

In the *Dog Day Afternoon* scene the asymmetry is shaped by the integration of
Dialogue Redundancy: Sonny's gleeful expressions of 'escape' occur twice.

There are occasions when the integration of beats and 'cinema naturalness'
dictate redundancies. This is especially true when either (or both) support the
emotional substance of the story.

TIP & HINT: Redundancies can be removed if they do 'nothing more' than replicate information distributed in another scene(s).

HINT & TIP: Visual Redundancy is a form of Visual Logic and Intercutting.
In the Amish Boy Spots the Killer scene from *Witness*, two 'identical' shots are used [*Figure 18.5*]: Samuel turns (twice) from the photo in the awards case, to 'catch' the attention of Detective John Book.

Figure 18.5

'Double' Dramatic Irony; 'Double' Tension

An SVA student used two takes of a little girl 'marching around' a laundromat; with doll in hand she touched each dryer. [*Figure 18.6*] This redundancy assisted in the beat construction — a 'break' was needed between two other beats — and the 'naturalness' of the setting: It would be peculiar if a child 'marched around' the laundromat only once!

Figure 18.6

Children love Redundancy

Brothers-In-Law
Director/Editor, Sabine Harbeke

The same student discovered a magnificent asymmetry for the Greenhouse scene in her thesis film, *June*:

INTERIOR. GREENHOUSE. DAY.

JUNE and MARIA dance about — celebrating MARIA'S plans to grow her own plants for her flower shop.

JUNE (dancing)
I'm going to have a child.

MARIA
(slowing her dancing and turning to JUNE)
What? No? You're kidding? You're not kidding...

From this scripted moment — and corresponding dailies — the student created:

INTERIOR. GREENHOUSE. DAY

In Long-Shot we see JUNE and MARIA dancing. A tape deck 'provides' music. Camera at their back.

JUNE *(dancing)*
I'm going to have a child.

MARIA *(sucking a tootsie pop)*
(slowing her dancing and turning to JUNE and the camera) [Figure 18.7]
What?

Figure 18.7

June
Director, Sabine Harbeke; Editor, Magnus Akten

Cut to: Close-Up. JUNE. She continues to dance. *[Figure 18.8]*

Figure 18.8

MARIA *(Off-Camera VO): No?*

JUNE *(Close-Up: dancing and dancing)*
I'm going to have a child.

Cut to: 'Opening' Long-Shot: [*Figure 18.9*]

Figure 18.9

MARIA (facing June and Camera)
You're kidding? You're not kidding...

June's secret 'revealed' twice, worked exceptionally.

Redundancy in the Greenhouse scene keys an integration of beats in 'code': Physical Action, Physical Life, Dialogue, Distribution Of Information; and Story, Place and Character(s).

HINT: The integration of Distribution of Information 'codes;' and Story, Place, and Character 'codes' exist in each scene used in this chapter.

An Alexander Calder sculpture supplies a visual analogy that 'displays' the ideas in this chapter. A Calder presents 'preferences in form' through diverse perspectives. It permits a personal touch that — from identical 'pieces' — creates an assortment of arrangements; the 'view' can 'change with the winds'; and a Calder is a 'scale' in balance. Its brilliance is asymmetry.

An extraordinarily simple — as inspired as a Calder — arrangement in asymmetry can be 'viewed' in the *Breaker Morant* sequence: the court's finding(s) and sentencing.

The sequence — some eight-plus scenes — discloses the court martial sentences with a gripping and diverse (asymmetrical) distribution of information; a masterful integration of Dialogue and Physical Action and Physical Life; vibrant contrasts of Interior and Exterior Place(s); [*Figure 18.10*] and...

Figure 18.10

...Compelling Reactions

HINT: The DNA/Dailies analogy reflects — as Walter Murch describes — each editor's excursion to 'distinguish' the 'just right' arrangement for a film.

lip
smacking
good

"Acting on stage is not the same thing as
acting before a camera. Only
later, in the cutting room, can any
authenticity be found."

— John Berger

Whenever I acquaint an editing class with my thinking on synchronized sound, I ask the students to tap the tops of their heads with one hand, and to simultaneously rub their tummies in a circular motion with the other. More often than not — to 'protect' students from such foolishness — I do it myself.

This bit of child's play reveals quickly and simply the relationship of sound — especially synchronized sound — to picture. At times I turn my back to the class and ask, "Am I speaking in sync?"

In 'real life' of course I am speaking in sync — what choice do I have — but if I'm in a film, and I turn my back... who knows? What if I cover my mouth when I speak? Am I in sync? In 'real life'? In film? If an actor's lips are not visible — and this is frequently the case: A Close-Up (Reaction) of another actor is on screen; an over-the-shoulder shot which does not reveal the lips of the speaker; or when dialogue is used as a transition to join scenes — the audience is viewing another Time or Place while hearing the continued dialogue. With each of these conditions the editor is free to assist, enhance, and (sometimes) to 'find' the actor's best performance.

HINT: When JUNE announced her secret — the camera was behind her —she was (actually) Out Of Sync. Her line was advanced, creating an extra beat before MARIA turned.

Frank Questions the Prisoner scene(s) from *Serpico*: This is a two scene sequence — it can be considered the opening two scenes of a six scene sequence.

HINT: More about Beats to Scenes to Sequences in a later chapter.

The first part — beat — of the first scene I'd call Frank Waits For the Prisoner. [*Figure 19.1*] Beat, scene, and sequence 'name calling' can assist the editor in the 'search' for structural arrangements.

Figure 19.1

TIP & HINT: Good 'name calling' is emotional and active

To dwell on this point a bit longer, the second part — final beat — of the first scene might be: Frank Takes the Prisoner for Coffee. The second scene ends with Frank Tries to Get the Prisoner to 'Snitch' beat.

This scene takes place in a newspaper/coffee shop, and 'begins' with dialogue played against Frank escorting the prisoner 'across the street' from the first scene. It would not be surprising for people in the audience to believe that Frank's last words were in sync. [*Figure 19.2*] Frank's back is to the audience — his mouth is unobserved, and lip synchronization isn't what's important.

Figure 19.2

FRANK: God damn shame you got to take this whole rap...

At that moment — barely on the word, "rap" — a cut takes us into the shop. At first — for half a beat — we see only the prisoner; Frank then emerges, [*Figure 19.3*] with a cup of coffee, as his body leans screen left.

Figure 19.3

...yourself

FRANK (continued)
I don't know, maybe you're guilty, maybe you're not. Maybe you just went along for the ride. I got a feeling you just went along...

Skip ahead several lines to the next essential moment for our topic:

FRANK
They're gonna put you away, you know that?

PRISONER
What can I get?

FRANK
Oh, let's see....

At this moment Frank looks off to screen right, and then back to the prisoner before a cut takes us to a Close-Up of the prisoner from over Frank's right shoulder. You will note that the prisoner's expression — eyes, and the posture of his head — is completely different [*Figure 19.4*] on either side of the cut. Our eyes however, could not resist 'catching' Frank's head in movement.

Figure 19.4

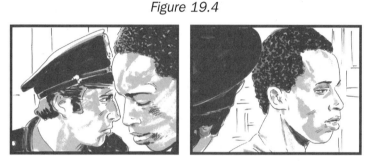

'Mismatch' is notable in still frames

FRANK
(continued; camera over right shoulder)
...kidnapping, sodomy, rape... are you kidding me...?

Throughout Frank's recitation of possible criminal charges, you can see — if you force yourself to take your eyes off of the prisoner — that Frank is 'out of sync.'

Actors working in theatre will often — no matter how many rehearsal sessions — discover that beats (or rhythms) need to be altered, or they might intuitively 'play' the discovery, and embrace it. During postproduction, the editor and director must 'find' the performance needs, and 'bring them about.' It may mean adjusting the pace; deleting lines; transposing lines; or, possibly using a preferred reading — in audio — of line(s) from one take, with the preferred picture from another, and 'syncing' the two.

TIP: It is far easier to sync elements from different takes by 'keying' the end of a line, or phrase. Disengage Picture and Sound. Listen to the line; stop at its end. Screen the Picture, reading the actor's lips — when you know the words, lip reading is a sure bet! Stop where the lips finish the phrase: It's easiest if you speak the words in your head. Both Sound and Picture end points are easily found if you relax, and stop from the normal (24fps or 30fps) speed. Lock Picture and Sound, and you're guaranteed — with very little practice — to be within a frame of 'precise' sync.

Here's another example of what might be called 'Out of Sync' but not 'Out of Kilter.'

Galvin Meets The Sister scene from *The Verdict*. [*Figure 19.5*] This is the INTERIOR OFFICE scene that follows the INTERIOR HALLWAY scene, mentioned in "It Beats Ticks & Tocks."

Figure 19.5

GALVIN: It's not a good case. It's a very good case.

Cut To:

GALVIN (over his right shoulder)
A young, healthy woman goes into the hospital to deliver her third child....

This second shot shows Galvin's client's sister. [*Figure 19.6*] She is seated on a couch; her body language discloses vulnerability, and sadness. Most important, we look at her — her face, her eyes. The composition's design makes her the focal point.

Figure 19.6

Galvin is out of sync, but who's looking?

Galvin's voice is the synchronized sound from his Close-Up — used initially in the scene. A cut in the Image does not necessitate a cut in the Sound; and the 'tummy rubbing' aspect of sound — its non-stop, non-staccato continuum — 'convinces' us of the moment to moment 'reality.'

TIP: When cutting dialogue there should be (many) more cuts in Picture than in Sound. You don't have to, and you shouldn't, try cutting across syllables, let alone into phrases wherever there's a cut in Picture. Those cuts are a dead give-away to the ear!

Cut To:

GALVIN
Well, it's just beyond comprehension... she's given the wrong anesthetic.

The third shot is a return to the first shot. Yes, Galvin is in sync! Galvin's dialogue has played across three shots.

At the outset of this scene, and prior to Galvin's first words, take note, and hear, an inhale. There is, as well, a very brief pause — beat — before the opening line is spoken.

HINT & TIP: It is not mandatory for a scene to begin with an immediate 'reading' of the first line of dialogue: It goes without saying that this is true for the last line of dialogue, and a scene's end. Dialogue should not propel a scene. Reactions/images and beats should be the editor's 'director.'

TIP: It is sometimes indispensable to deliberately 'throw' words out of sync. If a line of dialogue ends too close to an Outgoing Cut, a peculiar eye/ear sync discernment — the speakers' lips seem to have 'stopped' too soon — might require just 'that.' [*Figure 19.7*]

June provides such a situation: Games in the Flower Shop scene. June and Maria play 'I Can See Something.' Maria selects a 'something.' "And it's red!" June must guess what it is.

Figure 19.7

JUNE
Your earrings!

Cut To:

MARIA
They're not red, they're coral.

Cut To: Medium Long Shot over Maria's right shoulder.

MARIA
...and you ought to know that.

The word "that" ended some 1-2 frames before the Outgoing Cut of the Medium Long Shot. The Incoming cut was a return to MARIA'S Close-Up. It didn't work. There was a conspicuousness at the cut from the Medium Long Shot back to the Close-Up. It 'seemed' (initially) that the Medium Long Shot was altogether too quick. We made a tiny adjustment. When viewed again it 'appeared' that we had generously lengthened the shot, and that was why the cut now worked. But we had not adjusted the Medium Long Shot at all; we had added some 3-4 frames to the Incoming Close-Up of Maria — in Image only — allowing the eye to see Maria complete the word "that" [*Figure 19.8*] even though the word had already been 'said and done.' Yes, we were out of sync, but absolutely 'in kilter.' A persistent acuity to the ear, and an equivalent 'call' for visible 'life' in Maria's face, insisted on this adjustment.

"That" is 'perfectly' Out of Sync

HINT: Don't be certain too quickly about what's 'gone wrong,' and what 'fix' is needed.

However silly my 'head and tummy' classroom demonstration, it easily expresses the independence of Image from/and Sound. This independence is readily available: The Image and Sound are provided to the editor on separate elements — Picture and Magnetic Sound Track when editing on film, and as separate Video and Audio Tracks when editing digitally. Conceptual independence is indispensable if the editor expects to put the best finishing touches to his work.

HINT & TIP: The surest obstacles to creative film editing are the seduction of matching action, and the obsession with staying in sync.

The head tapping in my demonstration represents the film image as it is presented in staccato 'clicks' — add to the head tapping your imitation of a movie projector, and you'll 'get the picture.' The circular tummy rubbing represents the sound. Imagine the confounding difficulty technicians faced following the invention of sound recording: How can a talking picture be projected? If the head tapping were not the staccato projection of image, but rather a 'rendition' of dialogue playback, movies would have eve-ry-bo-dy/tal-king/li-ke/thi-s. And, if the tummy rubbing did not illustrate the ongoing flow of sound, but was rather a representation of the projected image, the movie audience would see perplexing streaks of blur — there'd be no pull down Stop/Start cycle in phase with a shutter mechanism — 'sliding' on the screen.

When dialogue recording became possible, two things became essential for post-production:

1. Image and Sound had to be situated on separate stock for the editor.
Without the capability to cut picture while not simultaneously cutting sound, and to cut sound while not simultaneously cutting picture, the editor would be forced to decide which one should be given preference; cuts would become a yielding to compromise, and not an artistic/creative choice.

2. Following completion in postproduction, a system had to be devised to join Image and Sound — 'marry' them on a single 'strip' of celluloid (a composite print) — for projection.

If films were shipped to theatres on separate elements, one of Image, and the other of Sound — Interlock Screenings, as in the editing room — there would be two distinct risks: If one element were damaged, and frames were 'lost,' the other element would have to be identically 'spoiled' in order to maintain synchronization; and there would be the ever-present concern that the projectionist might run non-corresponding reels — or the distributor, or laboratory might ship, print or incorrectly label various reels. Simply, a nine-reel movie would require 18 reels (nine of sound and nine of picture) and would greatly increase the likelihood of foul-ups.

This quandary led to the keeping of two elements while editing: Editorial Sync; and the producing of a single element for projection: Printer's Sync. In Editorial Sync the editor 'works' Pix and Sd in direct correspondence. Whether mechanical or digital, the Pix and Sd are kept 'alongside' each other — one above the other in the computer's Timeline configuration. There is no need for a Printer's Sync modification in Video or Digital 'projection.'

In Printer's Sync the final sound track is printed onto the edge of the picture, but to avoid having a staccato wavering in the audio, the laboratory prints the sound ahead of its corresponding frame of picture. This advance is 20 frames in 35mm, and 26 frames in 16mm. The looping of the film through the projector's configuration of spools allows for a 'tummy rubbing' action around the sound (pin-less) spool — 20 or 26 frames ahead of the corresponding picture — while at the same time a 'head tapping' action occurs in the gate/shutter mechanism, projecting the picture.

Image and Sound arrangements continue to be 'deliberated' as ever-perfecting innovations in digital sound and image advance. For the editor, creative obligations remain the same: Construct the scenes; craft the sequences; build a harmonious, and well (asymmetrically) balanced film.

TIP: It is tremendously advantageous to make use of the 'tummy rubbing' concept of sound, to assist in the unifying of cuts: Sound Effects; Ambience, Dialogue; Music; or any combination, can help provide 'convincing evidence' of 'real-life' Ongoing Time. Don't cut the Sound because you've made a cut in Picture; ambience — or any production recorded sound — from a preceding shot, should be carried across a cut, and 'play' (remain) until sync is (absolutely) needed. Often a cut will be perceived as 'wrong' when the ambient sound, cut at the very same moment, is troubling to the ear.

A Sequence from *Echoes*, an SVA thesis film, provides an example of how Out-Of-Sync Dialogue and 'Tummy-Rubbing' keep a cut together. Leslie and Marco Arrive at Her Mother's Farm: Jack, the mother's boyfriend, and farm hand, stops feeding the cattle when he sees Marco approaching the house. Two shots were joined for the Jack Hurries to the Farm House scene:

1. A Camera move takes us from a Close-Up of Jack's hands distributing hay, to a Medium Close-Up of Jack 'spotting' Marco, to a Medium Shot of Jack starting to walk hurriedly toward the house.
2. A Long Shot of Jack running toward the camera, and Marco.

Synchronized Dialogue was recorded for the second shot:

JACK
Hey! Hey! Can I help you?

The visual obviousness between Jack's hurried walk and his running presented a problem. [*Figure 19.9*] The choice solution was to 'distribute' the two
"Heys" on either side of the cut. The Incoming Long Shot was left intact; the
second "Hey!" and "Can I help you?" in actual sync. The first "Hey!" was
moved ahead to 'play' as Jack began his hurried walk. The camera is behind
Jack: No lips are seen.

Figure 19.9

HEY!   HEY! Can I help you?

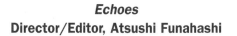
Echoes
Director/Editor, Atsushi Funahashi

HINT: When the lips of a speaking actor are not 'fully' visible, dialogue can be
deleted, rearranged from its original order, or the pacing can be altered. The editor must, when necessary, be able to 'influence' the performance rhythms.

There are times when, though no lips are on camera, dialogue readings will generate an actor's gesture of the head, arms, or hands; and such gestures 'convince' the editor that the filmed performance is 'locked.' But! Over the shoulder
shots offer more extensive 'influences' than might be realized.

In the over-the-shoulder shot from *Midnight Family Dinner* [*Figure 19.10*] Mary asks Joe, "How can you ask me a question like that?" Joe responds, "You're a prostitute!"

Figure 19.10

More adaptable than meets the eye

In one of my workshop classes it was agreed that Joe's response would 'play' far better if delayed for several beats more than in the dailies. With the camera behind Mary, we 'pulled' her line up, so that she finished "...me a question like that?" earlier, giving Joe 'more time' to react with his eyes — the class was fond of Joe's eyes — before answering. A problem came to light immediately: Mary made a strong gesture — her head nodding downward — on the opening word of her question, "**How**..."

The solution: We 'pulled' the line way up, so that Mary's strong nodding gesture was in 'sync' with "...**that**?" Joe had his long beat reaction/contemplation moment, just about equal to the total time it took Mary to ask her question.

TIP: Mary and Joe's dialogue reminds me that a cut from speaker to listener during 'hearty conversation' — anger, shouting/calling, broad (wide) mouth gestures — frequently demands Outgoing cuts at the moment of a 'full mouth': The mouth at, or near, 'wide open.'

Let's take Reactions Speak Louder Than Words a pace ahead. Take auditory notice of sound(s) made by a character who is on camera (reaction shot), while another character is speaking. In fact, you may 'notice' not a thing! It is surprising how seldom any of several 'life affirming' sounds are used. I have made it a point to gather inhales, exhales, and throat clearings — even chortles and giggles — to be selectively used 'with' non-speaking, or prior to speaking, characters. It provides an authentic 'feel' to dialogue. That is, characters appear, and sound — sometimes not on camera, but still sounding — as if they are fully 'alive' and so, fully listening — an important enhancing item in editing dialogue. It provides an additional sound layer, building genuineness in 'real-life' Ongoing Time.

There is no need for a DNA, tissue, or blood match. You can use a variety of such sounds randomly selected from different actors — the 'transplants' will seldom be 'rejected.'

Oh! And, lip smacking sounds? Gather them; they can be a most fitting addition to listener or speaker. Your mother's admonitions notwithstanding, lip smacking is good!

who could ask for anything more

> "All art constantly aspires towards the condition of music."
>
> — Walter Pater

Dr. Leonard Lionnet, in his forthcoming book *The Musical Eye: A Guide To Music For Filmmakers*, writes, "In early cinema, music was used to reduce the anxiety of a captive audience of strangers, within the dark, enclosed theatre."

Throughout film history, the moving image and music have been so readily fixed, each to the other, as to raise the likelihood, that from the outset, the movie house's piano accompaniment — in the silent film era — must have served as more than a 'plan' to muffle the projector's 'clickety-whirr.' Music 'soothingly' harmonizes the rhythmic character of juxtaposed images.

Sidney Lumet presented a simplification of all editing theory by declaring (perhaps he intoned) that good editing is "Nothing more than finding the right rhythms."

Editors keep 'click-tracks' (a form of cue track) on hand — a variety of music, or music-like recordings, usually with minimal, or no, melody, and unheard by an audience — to use (especially) when a scene, or larger structure, appears to evade rhythmic detection. Is there a more natural — or simple — way to divulge rhythm than through music — or musical elements?

Without a thought you'll tap your foot — a very natural reaction — to accompany music, and you'll find the beat that you are easily in sync with. If you were to give conscious thought to the music, you'd be able to be more selective: Slow down, or speed up, your tapping beats while continuing to be 'in sync' with the music. We have all heard various arrangements, and performances of a song, and while we might have a particular favorite, we can appreciate that several possibilities do work well.

I've described how beats provide an invaluable device for 'finding' scene and sequence structures. Beats get the editor to Tempo, or Pacing; and just as in a song, there are commonly several suitable arrangements. There is no singularly acceptable solution in the creation of a film — the editor is not 'looking for' the one and only rhythmic zenith — and that fact doesn't make for editing discord or strife. The reality, and a great editing quandary, is not that there is a one and only best answer, but that there are a great many potentially middling answers to rule out.

Ingmar Bergman said that he 'feels' his films are successful when "they are like a Bela Bartók symphony." Since Bergman didn't specify which film, or symphony, I'll take it to mean that his "successful" films 'match up' with different Bartók symphonies — perhaps even different Bartók arrangements.

A recent study has established a genetic connection — no formal music training is necessary — in humans that lets us immediately recognize discordant notes. In a way then, editors should be able to begin their careers with enormous potential: Being human — not chimps — they might be intuitively able to 'sense' flawed rhythms.

Finding Lumet's "right rhythm" is not exactly the same as 'hearing' a discordant measure. A musical note doesn't have to be an inept 'ping' to be detected as 'wrong.' It's a somewhat subtle proposition to 'create' just the right note, when no single note is a 'clinker.' The "right rhythm" in a film is to be discovered — don't discount that it is a rhythmic blend in image and sound — sandwiched somewhere between the intrinsic rhythm of a shot, and the emotional subtext(s) of a moment, a scene, a sequence, and the film's form. This is not necessarily a traditional two slices of bread sandwich, nor a three-slice club. How many slices is a question to be answered within the context(s) of the film.

TIP & HINT: The rhythms to be determined in a dialogue scene are about subtext. Understanding subtext is your guide to "the right rhythm." If possible, don't consider this an intellectual discovery of a film's theme(s) or message(s). Subtext is — best left — emotional. More about subtext in a few beats.

The most assumed remedy for getting to rhythm — as in tempo or pacing — is to make frequent, to very frequent, cuts; to 'hold' shots long, or very long; or to 'mathematically' calculate a series of shots, producing matching beats. These seldom work, because lots of cuts, or fewer cuts, have little to do with discovering effective rhythm. Realize that the number of frames from any one shot has little in common with the identical number of frames from another. What is significant is the 'busyness' of a (shot) composition — how quickly can our eyes place the focal point. This is often determined by whether the shot is an Establishing Shot; a Close-Up; whether the shot includes action, or is static; the influence of lens choices — the number and frequency of lens variations — which alter the eyes' perception of spatial relationships, and 'take' some eye 'fixing' time. Of course, what matters most is the combination of shots: Critical choices in the constructed order, and the eyes' familiarity with shots — how readily the eyes can recall an image.

Morant, Whitten, and Hancock Meet Major Thomas scene from *Breaker Morant* is made up of 44 cuts, which occur in two minutes — three of the cuts alone 'cover' 30 seconds. This is an unusually brisk tempo for a four character (dialogue) scene. Yet, the scene is neither frantic, nor chaotic in its rhythm(s). Five set-ups are used for the four characters. [*Figure 20.1*] Our eyes 'read' the shots quickly — they are limited, visually logical, and easily familiar.

Figure 20.1

Context ◄► Subtext ◄► Rhythm

HINT & TIP: I have used *Breaker Morant*, and this particular scene several times. Get to see the film; rent the tape or DVD. It is among the finest works; and serves as a significant learning 'tool.'

HINT: There is also something to be said for the way visual logic plays an unmistakable part in this scene: Physical Action motivates the Establishing (Master) Shot. The scene also offers a significant example of Rhythm/Subtext as cited in "Ask Gertrude Stein": in this case, questions 'unhappily' answered.

I have found that young editors — and students — are quick to sense that something is wrong with a grouping of shots whenever rhythmic conflict occurs. This may be proof of our innate abilities to catch a sour note, or two. What is worth mentioning is the inexperienced editor's often-inaccurate evaluation: He misinterprets the source of the 'sour note.'

Several years ago, a thesis student went nearly barmy by an adjustment I made to 'fix' a cut that he complained was 'off.' Following my effort, we screened four cuts leading up to, and including, the cut that troubled him.

HINT: It is of paramount importance to screen 'lead-up' moments — that might mean several dozen beats, or more — to any area that has proved 'disturbing,' or been recently 'retuned.' Not doing so would be the equivalent of a composer listening to but a single note: If there is no context, how can you find a 'right' rhythm?

"Ooh!" The student was elated. "You fixed the cut." I told him I hadn't touched the cut; that I had shortened a shot two cuts earlier. The student examined the trim I held in my hand. It wasn't the 16 or so frames from the shot he was certain was the culprit. He looked at me, and again at the trim — it was from the earlier shot. Skepticism showed in his eyes: He had witnessed editing 'magic'; or was it voodoo?

Louise Bryant Interviews Jack Reed scene from *Reds* gives us an example of Sync and Rhythm achievement — quite a bit of editing magic! The scene is commonly called the Coffee Cup scene. [*Figure 20.2*]

Louise asks about Jack's views on world politics, economics, and the recent outbreak of World War I. The dialogue for Jack's answers had not been written when the scene was shot; and so Jack paced back and forth 'improvising' declarations by number, "27...28...", to be 'fixed in the editing' with the later recorded dialogue. The scene 'plays' as an all night recitation over cup, after cup, after cup of coffee. At times Jack's voice segues upon itself.

Figure 20.2

Inventive Cutting: No Sync Dialogue and All Night Rhythms

HINT & TIP: If you don't get a "mental hiccup" at a 'troubling' cut, you can bet that you've 'heard' a rhythmic discord. The solution is frequently found several 'notes' back. You'll start to appreciate Sidney Lumet's counsel.

HINT: Remember that rhythm — as does visual logic — exists in an individual shot; and accordingly, an effective rhythm(s) might be found in any single cut: the sure impact of an Extreme Long Shot joined to an Extreme Close-Up.

Rhythm/Subtext:
It matters little that credible readings are provided by actors, you can still find yourself without dialogue. You'll do little more than begin to approach dialogue with a back-and-forth assembly of speaker and listener/responder. For dialogue to be truly 'correct' — rich and full and alive — it must possess emotional subtext.

It is not enough to know what a character says. Anyone reading the script could tell you that! The 'why' is what matters in both statement, and response, and reaction. And, if we know — or feel — the answers to these questions, what's rhythm got to do with it?

Maya Stops at the Store To Pay scene from *Nowhere, Now Here* gives a perfect example.

Maya — who has inherited a cottage in Finland from her great aunt — returns to the local grocery to pay for provisions she'd purchased earlier. Kaisa, the store clerk, had trusted her to "pay later."

MAYA *(holding money)*
I came to pay!

Maya hands the money to Kaisa.

MAYA *(continued)*
Did you know what my Great Aunt did for a living?
In one picture she looks like she was one tough lady.

KAISA
I think she ran a farm, and had some cows. Then
she sold the farm and moved to the cottage. That's
where she lived all year long for 30 years.

MAYA
It must be that Finnish sisu *I hear about!*

[*Sisu* is a Finnish expression meaning strength; toughness.]

KAISA
Must be. We're having a party tonight. You should come.
Anneli is making food, and there'll be lots of dancing.

The readings of the lines were reasonably credible. But, when cut together it was apparent that the scene was not in the 'right rhythm.' A couple of problems with subtext(s) — there was little to none — had to be remedied:

1. Maya did not come to the store only to pay. She wanted information about her great aunt. Although eager for answers, how quick — or bold — would she be to ask a (stranger) store clerk? How can that subtext be rhythmically interpreted?
2. Kaisa hardly knows Maya. Why would she invite her to a party? But, she does — read the script! How can we make this work? How can a rhythmic adjustment find the emotional subtext — or motivation?

The subtext of the first problem required at least a bit of a hesitation on Maya's part to take her from the Showing Her Honesty beat to the I Have a Question beat. This was simple to do: A pause was 'added' between the first of Maya's lines and the second "I came to pay" and "Did you know what my Great Aunt...?" A shot of Kaisa, putting the money into the register added one beat, and a cut back to Maya — allowing her actual, though very brief, pause between her lines — added another beat. During the extra beats, the audience can 'read' Maya's face: She is here for something else; and she is uncomfortable, and hesitant.

HINT: Thinking/Feeling: The audience wants to know, "What is it?" This is so much better than "Can I ask you a question?"

The rhythmic interpretation to establish a subtext for the second 'problem' required a little more dramatic insight, and finesse.

Kaisa's lines — in response to "It must be that Finnish *sisu* I hear about" — were correct, but in recitation only. Dramatically, it seemed necessary to have Kaisa take delight in Maya's effort at Finnish vernacular. Her amusement would motivate the party invitation. An outtake was found in which the actress playing Kaisa missed a line, and began to laugh. Her laughing face formed just the 'right' emotional subtext beat. A cut back to a smiling Maya demonstrated pleasure in making comfortable contact. [*Figure 20.3*] Only then does Kaisa offer the wel-coming — to her Finnish village — party invitation.

Figure 20.3

Joyful Company ←→ Community ←→ Invitation

TIP: Never rule out anything from the uncut dailies. Every moment between the slate and the camera's stop holds promise.

I once used a shadowy figure moving past the camera to make a cut work. The 'figure' was a member of the production crew exiting screen right after 'clapping' the slate to mark that synchronized sound take.

I'm sure that you'll be astounded by the (exaggerated) asymmetry in the rhythms of the Killer Looks Through the Restroom Stalls beat from *Witness*. [*Figure 20.4*] The search from stall to stall to stall, at first glance and note, 'seems' rhythmically consistent — as in balanced, symmetrical; (nearly) no one believes otherwise — but, with smart reflection, a 'feel' for context, emotional subtext, and most definitely in storyshowing inspiration, the editing choice brilliantly enhances the beat(s), and scene.

Figure 20.4

Asymmetry in the rhythms of sound and action

HINT: Film rhythms are not metronome precise — and needn't be. Asymmetry applies!

i have
my
doubts

"I don't think a finished film is ever anything that anybody envisions initially."

— Evan Lottman

When I was nine years old, and an enthusiastic 'artist,' a cousin — he was much older, and I thought of him as an uncle — who, as an avocation, enjoyed painting, took me on an afternoon excursion to Greenwich Village. I was enlivened by New York City's celebrated neighborhood of artists and writers; and elated by my cousin's purchase of oil paints, brushes, palette, linseed oil, turpentine, and a few pre-stretched canvases as a gift for me.

My parents — my mother especially — kindly tolerated the overpowering odor of linseed oil and turpentine in our small New York City apartment. I remember the delectable ecstasy the first time I applied a creamy thick dab of oil color to my canvas. The color was yellow, and it coated the outside wall of a farmhouse I copied — first sketching in pencil — from an illustration I found in a magazine.

I was so captivated by the work that I would get out of bed in the middle of the night — even during the school week — to sneak into the bathroom with my art supplies, so that I could continue my painting. The bathroom was the only room in our apartment to afford privacy: It had a door. I worked carefully toward my anticipated achievement.

When the landscape was completed, I was left with a disappointing canvas. I had worked with a fastidious certainty — a consequence of creative innocence; and my painting — unlike the illustration I copied — was lifeless and flat. More accurate: It was flat, and therefore lifeless.

There's a phrase about a "surface not even begun to be scratched" that comes to mind whenever I recall my first oil painting. The expression implies the existence of something more than a surface.

I bought a book about Rembrandt van Rijn, and made a stupendous discovery: Rembrandt didn't fill in his drawn lines with final color! Instead, he created a broad and lively spontaneity of 'washes' in muted to bright hues. He crafted the canvas in its entirety. Rembrandt did not, from the outset, resort to a finicky rendering of one object, before moving on to the next. Unlike the way I had proceeded to paint my yellow house, solid in color, and void of texture, as if painting an interior wall, Rembrandt encouraged the energetic under-painting to show through — perhaps even provoking 'missteps' in his search for fullness in breadth and form.

Francis Bacon wrote, "If a man will begin with certainties, he shall end in doubts, but if he will be content to begin with doubts, he shall end in certainties." Mr. Bacon is addressing a philosophy in the search for contentment. But! The 'play' between doubt and certainty is an imperative in the creative process.

Orson Welles defined a director as "Someone who presides over accidents." Sidney Lumet said, "All good work is the result of accidents." Walter Murch poetically describes the creative process, for the film editor, "editing is not so much a putting together as it is a discovery of a path."

Scratch the surface of these comments, and you'll make a stupendous discovery: Creativity can, and will, be bared by way of doubt — or 'holding back' certainty!

TIP: The work process should allow — should even foster — the often-extraordinary discovery. Try to develop a knack for not working too cautiously, to letting things happen. The result can be serendipitous, giving you invaluable insights and a terrific new perspective.

Murch writes about his efforts — with several co-editors — to 'find' the final form for *Apocalypse Now*: He calculated the total number of days of work, and the number of cuts in the finished film, and came up with 1.47 cuts per day, per editor. The answer might seem altogether non-productive, but only if the editors arrived to work knowing exactly what single cut (and then some) to make before heading back home. While Apocalypse Now is likely an exaggerated example of "a discovery of a path," it does demonstrate the many cuts discarded before a 'final arrangement' is made!

Early in the book, I suggested that the editor's "definitive achievement" is not to be found in any single cut, but in the "unity of the entire film." If, in the post-production process, more than 90% of your initial cuts lead — in the end — to 'somewhere else', why proceed with a 'finicky' first cut?

I am not advocating an altogether 'hit and miss' approach, as Welles, Lumet, and Murch are not speaking about work of slapdash drifting. There is a practical side to the methodology of the creative process. The editor's (filmmaker's) handling of the groundwork — under-painting — is orderly, and can be resourcefully productive.

Digital technology — Final Cut Pro software — presents me a bond between my painting past to editing's future. The program display features two screens: Viewer and Canvas. The Canvas 'plays' your 'picture in progress.'

This chapter is about the editor's canvas! The path to discover sequences.

In the thesis film, *June*, a nighttime scene, June Telephones Her Father, originally followed the daytime scene, June Arrives at Maria's Flower Shop. You can probably guess from this writing that it was deleted. There was a (harmful exposition) redundancy in the two scenes — though they were not sequential: June 'tells' her father that she's returned from London, and will be coming to see him.

Some half-dozen scenes following the Telephone scene was the June Asleep on Her Father's Boat scene. Deleting June's father earlier 'kept' the audience from 'seeing' the father, and hearing June announce her return from London — we've already learned this in the Maria's Flower Shop scene — and her plans. This new arrangement furthered the audience's curiosity when June's father 'finds' her asleep on his boat, [*Figure 21.1*] and the structure now 'kept' June and Maria together in the next three scenes.

Figure 21.1

Who Is This Guy?

TIP: No matter how effective any, or all, scenes might be they don't fully serve the needs of the complete film if you don't find sequences. When an entire film — or a portion of a film — 'feels' sporadic, it is likely the result of an editing focus on scenes. This often leads to observably episodic, and poorly integrated, storytelling.

The 'right' questions can get you to some bright discoveries in sequence structuring.

Jerry Tries To Call Off the Kidnapping scene from *Fargo*: Jerry asks the mechanic in the auto dealership's service department for help in 'calling off' the abduction of his wife. [*Figure 21.2*] The mechanic 'plays' ignorant of the plot, and any previous involvement. Jerry walks away.

Figure 21.2

Scene in an awkward position

The next scene — sequentially — reveals Carl and Gaear entering Minneapolis. What if the audience witnessed the Carl and Gaear scene first? Structured in reverse, the audience would know the kidnappers have already arrived in Minneapolis [*Figure 21.3*]...

Figure 21.3

...and Jerry is trying to stop them

It makes more sense that way. Why? We know from the 'mechanic scene' that Jerry can't stop the kidnapping. To follow with a scene that 'says' the kidnappers haven't been stopped, is superfluously non-dramatic. But reversed...?

What if, at the end of the scene with the mechanic, Jerry didn't walk away? What if the mechanic were not so definite in his denying help to Jerry? What if the audience believes that the mechanic is going to help? Or is unsure? What if the audience did not 'see' Carl and Gaear entering Minneapolis? What impact would that have at the outset of the Kidnappers Appear at Jerry's House scene? [*Figure 21.4*]

Figure 21.4

HINT: Stronger by deletion

Paul Hirsch explained that "sometimes the biggest contribution I've made [editing] a film is taking a scene out. Take that out and everything flows..."

What if the kidnapping has already occurred before the Jerry Tries To Call Off the Kidnapping scene?

I am not asking these questions to motivate an intellectual examination. 'See' if the questions — and your skill at visualization — might stir answers in emotion.

Students — and inexperienced editors — fluctuate between being satisfied too quickly, and being discouraged too easily. Both are a result of an inclination to evade uncertainty. Doubt can be creatively gratifying!

TIP: Full discovery won't arrive with answers. Don't be (so) certain before you do the cuts; do the adjusting; 'see' what your labors bring; and how the doing illuminates your "discovery of a path."

"Laziness" is the editor's worst offense, said Dmytryk. He was not referring to snoozing.

The Verdict: From the 'discovery' of a missing admitting nurse — Who's Nurse Rooney Protecting scene — through the Galvin Telephones the Admitting Nurse scene, there is an eight-scene sequence [*Figure 21.5*] that is 'driven' by...

Figure 21.5

...Galvin's 'detective work'

As each scene 'plays out,' the audience feels an increasing 'need' to inhale: An emotional balloon is incrementally inflated. The audience — and even Galvin — holds its breath when the nurse identifies herself in Galvin Telephones the Admitting Nurse scene. A two-scene sequence — Galvin at Logan Airport and Laura's Going to New York [*Figure 21.6*] — 'shows the way' to the Galvin Confronts the Admitting Nurse scene.

Figure 21.6

Hold your breath or exhale

A sequence might be identified by purely visual associations which can connect one scene to the next; by unbroken emotional expansion established by particular inflections, either emotional and/or narrative: the mood or tone of ordered scenes, and/or their distribution of information.

If, in *The Verdict*, Galvin's two visits to funeral parlors were structured consecutively — rather than (as exists in the finished work) separated by the Galvin and the Obituary Page scene [*Figure 21.7*] — the tone of the sequence would be strikingly altered: Near amusing pathos would replace the (far better) discomforting down-and-out pathos.

Figure 21.7

Tone Matters!

The Philadelphia Train Station scenes in *Witness* make up three sequences —
supported by tone and inflection — even though they exist continually, and in the
same 'Place.' Sequence #1 [*Figure 21.8*] begins with a Master Shot of the
Station Mezzanine scene, and runs through the High Angle Shot of the Samuel
Explores the Station scene.

Figure 21.8

Sequence #2 [*Figure 21.9*] begins with the Mother and Samuel Sit in the Waiting Area scene — the last note of music from the preceding scene carries into the new (sequence) inflection; and in this case, time — and runs through the Samuel in the Restroom scene.

Figure 21.9

Sequence #3 begins — and might end — with the Mother and Samuel are Surrounded by the Police scene. Or, the sequence [*Figure 21.10*] might consist of two scenes...

Figure 21.10

...Second: John Book Arrives scene

Certain delineations — fades; dissolves; postproduction sound effects and music; specific beats and actions — may well generate 'disagreements' in sequence identification. Don't fret! It's just one more doubt.

A sequence might be 'broken down' into a mini-sequence; music spotting, sound effects, or dialogue, can precede — and introduce — an upcoming sequence.

HINT & TIP: Music and other sounds 'play' a vital part in the 'bringing together.' They offer a simple, yet essential, approach to 'hide' the episodic — fragmented — nature of film scenes to sequences. And isn't inconspicuous harmony what we're 'looking for'?

No external record — as in a theatrical performance playbill — 'specifies' scenes, sequences, or acts. More often than not — in the end — editing doubts come to this:

> "*And then, one fine day, when we somehow managed to devise one last, desperate rearrangement — there was the film.*"
>
> — Andrey Tarkovsky

dear reader

"Film Editors are the finest people I know.
I don't think I've ever met an editor
I didn't like. They're the most wonderful,
dedicated, hard-working people...."

— Tina Hirsch

During my semester-long sabbatical — completing work on this book — I continued to meet with my thesis students at SVA. On one of those days, I arrived early, and brought my bagel and cup of coffee into the foyer of the Digital Imaging Center. The Center is often available for twenty-four-hour student bookings; and can be counted on to be among the first facilities opened each morning. A student behind the counter greeted me, "Good morning," and asked if I were a teacher. I said, "Yes. Though not in the Digital Imaging Center, but in Room 504, next door." She inquired instantly, "Are you a Final Cut Pro teacher?" FCP is an Apple software program that allows for digital editing on a computer. Room 504 has become an impressive lab with well over a dozen FCP workstations. I hesitated — not because I didn't know whether to declare, "Yes" or "No," but because the student's question pointed out a profound change in perceptions of teaching, and learning. My pause made her begin to suspect that I had sneaked in past security, to eat my breakfast sheltered from the cold morning. I replied, hardly a moment before the student was going to ask for ID, "Not too many years ago, Room 504 housed Steenbecks, and no one ever asked me if I was a Steenbeck teacher." I didn't ask if the student referred to her Graphic Design teacher as the Photoshop teacher.

It did cross my mind several years ago, that one of the mainstay adages of work world crafts, "Learning the tools of the trade," has — for the most part — been rearranged to "Learning the tool of the trades."

New technologies, and their trade-promoting vocabulary, induce — in me at least — some discomfort: I am ill at ease with digital editing's designation as Non-Destructive. I know of no film editor who feels that his or her labors have ever been destructive. The reference's conceit is as unbecoming as the phrases Computer Illiterate and Information Age.

Such 'self-praising' phrases are bigheaded: They express a disregard — in their belittling — of earlier eras, and craftsmen. In this, they do nothing less than reject history, and the possibility that 'yesteryear' and 'yesterpeople' can contribute valuable instruction.

In large part this reflects the marketing strategies of Madison Avenue: Ted Widmer, the director of the C. V. Starr Center for the study of the American Experience at Washington College, wrote, "youth means money in Ponce de León's America." The young and carefree are 'with it' and 'where it's at'; and by inference, elders — even our wisest — are 'unfashionably elsewhere.' There is irony here: The 'young and carefree' are (perpetually) 'consuming' their dear days on the road to 'elsewhere'!

Digital editing offers brilliantly lovely work methods and strategies. I've adapted my editing 'habits' to take full — and then some — advantage of digital's offerings. While a digital editing 'machine' is a tool, it does as all tools do, offer an 'addendum': Encounters with any work paraphernalia can't help but encourage particular methods, and perhaps even results! This fact is worthy of an entire dissertation, but for now, I'll only raise one question: Does digital editing 'deter' the editor from spending 'creative time' in uncertainty?

Editors can now immediately 'soften' a cut with a dissolve; they can add an assortment of other optical effects, vast selections of sound effects, and music; and they can create near-instant titles — many dazzlingly sophisticated. All the finishing touches can be accomplished in remarkably short time. My concern — and a very large risk to the art of film editing, and moviemaking's future — is that all the feasibly elaborate finishing touches can so easily disguise barely mediocre work.

At a time when about 10%-20% of feature films were being cut on digital equipment, I was able to identify Avid or Lightworks — at the time, the two most widely-used digital tools — edited films. Whenever I suspected that this was so, I'd wait through the end credits, and sure enough, some acknowledgment would appear indicating a digital editing tool. To be fair, and honest, I'll admit that I didn't stay for the end credits of all films; and I am certain that some of the features I saw were edited digitally, but didn't 'raise my suspicions.' And, of course, I am not saying that every mechanically edited film guaranteed a job well done.

So many contemporary films are overly symmetrical (in part) because of digital editing. Though considered 'nonlinear' the tool encourages linear work habits and techniques. This easily leads to symmetry in work, and product. Could this have something to do with the naming, and design, of the Timeline?

Well over a decade ago I was invited to 'have a look' at an early version of Avid. The representative — a polite and helpful gentleman — demonstrated on a 'tutorial' available at the time. He began with a Long Shot of a sailing yacht, manned by a crew of a dozen or so, each wearing bright yellow or orange slickers. Then he made a cut to a Medium Shot which focused attention on the helmsman. I thought — but said nothing — that I would have intuitively arranged the shots the other way around: the Medium Shot first.

The cut didn't work. The 'editor' knew it didn't work. He said so. He didn't know why — he didn't try to guess, nor ask me if I knew. I did, but in the interest of courtesy — I wanted to be respectful; I did appreciate the 'lesson' — I offered (only) my agreement that the cut didn't work. It didn't work because by sheer bad luck, the moment of the Outgoing cut was made just as a crewman in a yellow slicker gestured with his arm; and in response to this movement our eyes 'darted' to him, just as the Incoming cut showed us the helmsman in an orange slicker — we had a 'mental hiccup'.

The solution proposed, and immediately completed, was to 'select' a dissolve across the cut. I thought to myself, "Ouch!"

Every optical effect — from traditional fades and dissolves, to split and swirling Images — adds beats to a film; and may 'wound' the moments preceding, and/or proceeding the effect: We might regard these as 'Placebo Effects' at best; or worse, 'Sugar Beats.'

Film editing is an interpretive art. The editor is the 'interpreter' of other interpretive artists: Director, Cinematographer, Production Designer, Actor, and (at times) Writer. This simple guiding principle is, and always will be, tool-free!

HINT: I'm beginning to feel my bond to Eisenstein's *The Old and the New*!

I encourage you to take full advantage of the new technologies, but work as though they were 'yesteryear machines.' Until ever-newer technology provides you a computer key that reads, Make This A Beautiful Movie, don't let your tools 'hide' your failings; have them 'lend a hand' in your "discovery of a path."

We confront a critical distinction: Easy is not the same thing as simple. The new technologies make it easy to confuse the two. Editing is not, nor should we expect it to be, easy. Editing is, and should remain, simple.

Many years ago I caught a few minutes of a documentary on PBS. The final scenes were of an international competition of ballet dancers hoping to be signed by prestigious companies. When I turned on the television, a young ballerina was nearly to the end of her performance. Gracefully completing her work, she glided to the wings at stage left, to enthusiastic applause, and shouts of "Bravo." A second camera caught the 'backstage' action: The dancer collapsed — physically resembling Raggedy-Ann — into her coach's arms. She gasped so horribly for breath, that if you were to hear her sound alone, you might expect that it was a snoring drunk.

The applause continued, and her coach lifted her, and pushed her back toward the stage, and another bow. The 'near-death' dancer instantaneously became, once again, the graceful ballerina, soaring to accept the unending ovation — she was feather-light on her toes, her arms elegant above her head. She acknowledged the audience, glided smartly off to the wings, and for a second time became the snoring drunken Raggedy-Ann.

Ballet, I thought, is not easy. I could tell from the images caught by the backstage camera. But, I thought, ballet is simple, beautifully simple. I could tell from the orchestra camera.

Editing, whether on film, electronic, or digital, does not demand a ballerina's athleticism, or quite the abundance of grace. A willingness to perform dedicated work may not be comparable to the dancer's 'death-defying' 'trial' in training and performance, but the film editor and ballerina do share an essential requirement: A presentation, before an audience that amazes in its simplicity, while 'keeping secret' all the labor, struggle, and experience that were central to each moment on stage, or screen.

There have been moments when I have felt enormously contented with my understanding and skill. You'll be amazed yourself, when you get to 'see' an ever broader, and richer perspective, while advancing in abilities to simplify. These moments are good — they do provide reassurance, and confidence in my teaching, and less anxiety at the start of a new project. Well, a little less anxiety anyway.

I know — the writing of this book supplied the proof, if proof were needed — that all those precious moments add up to a humbling, although strangely satisfying fact: Understanding and skill — even raw talent — continue to progress and develop. All you have to do is give of your time and your effort; but be certain that you maintain (at least) a little 'doubt.' Understanding and skill are very much like a pair of favorite blue jeans. With the wearing and washing they continue to get closer and closer to that 'perfect fit' — and 'feel.' One morning when you put them on, positive that they've finally 'arrived,' a knee rips through!

There is a reason — or two — that postproduction technologies have been researched, developed, and designed, to duplicate — so as to replace — what a 'yesterperson' film editor did, needed to do, or have done by someone else. So yes! There are lots of new tools to learn, and you should start today. There is far more than that to be learned for tomorrow, if you're willing to take a look at yesterday. I have packed this book with many of my yesterdays.

I have offered what I know about film editing. I also know that starting tomorrow, we can all look forward to lots more learning.

about the author

Richard D. Pepperman lives in Monmouth County, NJ & Mount Holly, VT.

Credits include:

Co-Editor, *The Boy from New Orleans: A Tribute to Louis Armstrong*.

Editor, *Touch: The Domain of the Senses*, Official Entry, Sitges Film Festival.

Consulting Editor, *Five Wives, Three Secretaries & Me*. Honored by the Academy of Motion Picture Arts & Sciences as one of the Outstanding Documentaries of 1999.

Consulting Editor: *Say It Isn't So*, Official Entry, Rotterdam Film Festival.

Production/Post Production Advisor: *Echoes*, Official Entry, Munich Film Festival. Karlovy Vary Film Festival.

Screenwriting Judge: Nicholl Fellowships; Academy of Motion Picture Arts & Sciences.

Supervising Editor: Promotional Music Videos, Columbia Records, *The Music People*.

Editor on more than 1000 commercial spots, including Postproduction Supervisor, *Barrier Free Design*: PSA Spot; Andy Award.

Designed and conducted editing workshops and seminars at Film/Video Arts, Pratt Institute, and The New School University.

Richard is a teacher and thesis advisor at the School of Visual Arts, where he was honored with the Distinguished Artist-Teacher Award.

bibliography

Achenbach, Joel. "Doctor, My Eyes. How we watch TV ads."
National Geographic, vol. 203, no. 2 (February 2003).

Bergman, Ingmar. *Images: My Life in Film*
New York: Arcade Publishing, 1990.

Dancyger, Ken. *The Technique of Film & Video Editing*
Boston: Focal Press, 1993.

Dmytryk, Edward. *On Film Editing: An Introduction to the Art of Film Construction*
Boston: Focal Press, 1984.

Eisenstein, Sergei. *Film Form: Essays in Film Theory and The Film Sense*
Cleveland & New York: Meridian Books, 1957.

Eisenstein, Sergei. *Towards a Theory of Montage, Volume 2*
London: BFI Publishing, 1991.

Kasdan, Margo A., Christine Saxton and Susan Tavernetti. *The Critical Eye: An Introduction to Looking at Movies*
Dubuque, Iowa: Kendall/ Hunt Publishing, 1988.

Kyrou, Adonis. *Luis Buñuel*
New York: Simon & Schuster, 1963.

LoBrutto, Vincent. *Selected Takes: Film Editors on Editing*
New York: Praeger, 1991.

Mamet, David. *On Directing Film*
New York: Viking Penguin, 1991.

Murch, Walter. *In the Blink of an Eye: A Perspective on Film Editing. 2nd Edition*
Los Angeles: Silman-James Press, 1995.

Oldham, Gabriella. *First Cut: Conversations with Film Editors*
Berkeley: University Of California Press, 1992.

O'Steen, Sam. *Cut to the Chase: Forty-Five Years of Editing America's Favorite Movies*
Studio City, CA: Michael Wiese Productions, 2001.

Tarkovsky, Andrey. *Sculpting in Time*
Austin: University of Texas Press, 1989.

Wohl, Michael. *Editing Techniques with Final Cut Pro*
Berkeley: Peachpit Press, 200

filmography

The Accidental Tourist
Alexander Nevsky
Alicia Was Fainting
Amadeus
Atlantic City
Breaker Morant
Brothers-in-Law
Burnt by the Sun
Catch-22
Chinatown
Colonel Redl
The Color Purple
The Crucible
Dead End
Dersu Uzala
Dog Day Afternoon
The Domain of the Senses
Echoes
Fargo
The 400 Blows
The French Connection
Jack Murphy
Joe Gould's Secret
The Joy Luck Club
June
Law & Order
Leaving Las Vegas
Life Before Me
Little Big Man
The Loneliness of the Long Distance Runner
Midnight Family Dinner
Nowhere, Now Here
The Painter
Pascali's Island
Reds
Rosemary's Baby
Serpico
sex, lies, and videotape

Straight Story
Strike
The Sweet Hereafter
Touch
The Treasure of the Sierra Madre
The Trip to Bountiful
The Verdict
The Virgin Spring
Witness

index

A

accident(s), 217

Accidental Tourist, The, 111-114

acting, 35, 45, 66, 112, 114, 115, 154, 160, 163, 171, 174, 178, 179, 191, 194, 196, 203, 212, 230. *See also* performance

action, 15, 209, 214. *See also* cutting on action

action transitions, 68

actor. *See* acting

actress. *See* acting

Adams, Henry, 158

Akten, Magnus, 105, 189

Alexander Nevsky, 27, 101

Alexandrov, G.V., 154

Alicia Was Fainting, 16-17

allegory, 174

Allen, DeDe, xvii, 144, 165

all-purpose time, 105, 107, 108

Amadeus, 59-61, 162, 172, 185

ambience. *See* ambient sound

ambient sound, 29, 202. *See also* silence; roomtone

America(n), 144, 228

anagram, 137, 139, 140

analogy, 182, 190, 191

answer(s), 172-177, 179, 204, 208-210, 212, 213, 217, 220

anticipation, 165, 167, 177

Apocalypse Now, 217

art. *See* artists

artists, 74, 141, 144, 207, 216, 229, 230

asymmetry, 26, 27, 55, 76, 79, 104, 108, 183-186, 190, 202, 214

Atlantic City, 75, 77, 94, 95, 123, 126

audio, 156, 160, 165, 169, 183, 184, 196, 200

Avid, 229. *See also* computer; digital technology; Final Cut Pro; Lightworks

B

Bacon, Francis, 216

ballet, 9-11, 230, 231

Bartók, Bela, 208

beat(s), 17, 28, 30-40, 41, 43-45, 55, 58-60, 62, 64, 68, 100, 133, 139, 147, 149-151, 100, 133, 139, 147, 149-151, 160, 161, 163, 165, 166, 175-178, 184-186, 188, 190, 194-196, 198, 204, 208, 209, 211, 213, 214, 224, 230

Berger, John, 193

Bergman, Ingmar, 153, 208

Berle, Milton, 3

Bertolucci, Bernardo, 99

Bicycle Thief, The, 105

Big Chill, The, 79

blur, 7-8, 11, 201. *See also* imbalanced blur

bow, 114-119

Breaker Morant, 30, 115, 116, 126, 127, 168, 176, 177, 184, 185, 190, 191, 209, 210

Brothers-In-Law, 188

Brownell, Ian, 84

Brunet, Michel, 182

Bryant, Louise, 211

Buñuel, Luis, 1

Burke, James Lee, 181

Burnt By the Sun, 41, 42, 43, 161

C

Calder, Alexander, 190

Callas, Maria, 95

camera placement, 112, 115. *See also* set-ups

canvas, 216, 217

Catch-22, 77

celluloid triacetate, 111, 201

certainty, 216, 229, 231

Chandler, Raymond, 103, 148, 154

character, 49, 56, 74, 76, 77, 79, 93-95, 97, 111-113, 119, 126, 132, 149, 158, 160, 167, 168, 172, 174, 179, 182, 190, 204, 212

Chinatown, 94, 95

chronology, 84, 100

cinematography, xvii, 160, 230

cinema naturalness, 186

click-tracks, 208. *See also* cue tracks

codes, 182-186, 190

coding, 136

cognitive, 3, 11, 158, 159

collaboration, xiv, 92, 136
Colonel Redl, 7
Color Purple, The, 79, 80
Columbia Pictures, 165
composer, 136, 211
composite print, 201
compressing action, 15. *See also* action, cutting on action
computer, 162, 228. *See also* Avid; digital technology; Final Cut Pro; Lightworks
computer illiterate, 228
conflict, 129, 130, 136, 140, 156, 210
contemplation, 165, 167, 204
context, 68, 76, 122, 123, 125-127, 130, 136, 146, 149, 165, 166, 176, 182,
        185, 210, 211, 214
Continuing Ed, 100, 182
contrast, 102
convincing material, 157, 158
creation, xv, 22, 39, 71, 108, 127,178, 181, 189, 190, 194, 200, 201, 208,
        209, 216, 217, 220, 229
credits, 66, 229. *See also* titles
cross-cutting, 66, 67, 74-76, 79
Crucible, The, 36, 37, 38, 39, 43, 44, 149, 175, 176
cues, 158
cue track, 208. *See also* click-track
cut away, 92-94, 97
cuts, 6; bad, 6-8; compressing time, 15; discernible, 6, 16; good, 6, 8, 14; jump
        cuts, 24, 28-30; over-cutting, 59, 74. *See also* extended cuts
cutting on action, 7, 9, 14-16, 18, 20-22

D
dailies, 34, 66, 90, 124, 136, 157, 158, 160, 164, 177, 182, 189, 191, 214
DAT recording, 66
Day-Lewis, Daniel, xvii
Dead End, 105-108
definite time, 105-108
Denver, John, 51
Dersu Uzala, 108
dialogue, 14, 19, 35, 41, 49, 56, 57, 59-61, 63, 66, 92, 112, 116, 135,
        147-150, 154, 157, 160, 163, 165, 167, 168, 176, 182-186, 190,
        191, 194, 195, 198, 199, 201-204, 209, 211, 212, 217, 224
digital technology, 34, 136, 200, 201, 217, 228, 229, 231. *See also* Avid;
        computer; Final Cut Pro; Lightworks

Q

questions, 87, 130, 163, 172-177, 179, 204, 209, 212, 213, 218, 220, 228, 229

R

radio, 154

reactions, 37, 38, 150, 160-162, 167-169, 176, 177, 179, 191, 194, 198, 204. *See also* double reactions

real-life associations, 37, 134, 157, 194, 202

real world experiences, 130

Reds, 211

redundancy, 155, 165, 186-188, 190, 218

Reed, Jack, 211

Rembrandt, 216

rhythm, 23, 35, 36, 45, 104, 135, 147, 160, 165, 172, 177, 179, 196, 203, 208-214,

roomtone, 29. *See also* silence; ambient sound

Rosemary's Baby, 38, 39, 137-140

rough cut, 66, 166

rushes. *See* dailies

S

Schoonmaker, Thelma, xvii

School of Visual Arts (SVA), xiv, 2, 122, 135, 162, 188, 202, 228

Scorsese, Martin, xvii

screenplay, 35, 56, 90, 92, 93, 97, 100, 103, 106-108, 135, 144, 148, 149

screenwriter. *See* screenplay

script, 84, 92, 108, 134, 135, 139, 158, 212

Sculpting In Time, 34. *See also* Tarkovsky

segue, 211

Selected Takes: Editors On Editing, 165. *See also* Lobrutto, Vincent

selected takes, 34, 45, 66, 67

sequence, 14, 39, 41, 42, 90, 100, 108, 122, 130, 132, 156, 172, 174, 190, 191, 194, 202, 208, 209, 217, 218, 221-225

Serpico, 22, 23, 68, 69, 84-86, 161, 173, 194-196

set-ups, 14, 15, 19, 28, 57, 58, 100, 112, 164, 179

sex, lies, and videotape, 76

Shaw, George Bernard, 121

Shimokawa, Akira, 178

shutter, 201, 202

Sight & Sound, xvii

silence, 29. *See also* ambient sound; roomtone

Texaco Star Theatre, 3
theatre, 37, 38, 92, 120, 149, 150, 154, 160, 178, 185, 196, 201, 208, 225
theory, xv, xvii, 22, 124, 182, 208
three dimensions, 10, 100, 111, 113, 114, 120
time, 33, 36-38, 41, 76-79, 95, 96, 100-102, 106, 108, 150, 158, 174, 194, 209, 224, 229, 231. *See also* emotional time/duration; structuring time
time left out, 103
timeline, 229
titles, 66, 104, 229. *See also* credits
Toklas, Alice B., 174
tools, x, 34, 35, 228-231. *See also* Avid; computer; digital technology; Lightworks; Moviola; Steenbeck
Touch, 135, 136, 140, 141
Treasure of the Sierra Madre, The, 120
trial, 174
Trip to Bountiful, The, 51-53, 57-59, 166
Truffaut, Francois, 70
two dimensions, 14, 111

V
vanishing point perspective, 110
VCR, 6, 100, 154
Verdict, The, 26, 27, 40, 41, 89, 92, 115-119, 125, 173, 197, 198, 221-223
vernacular, 213
VHS, 48, 154. *See also* tape
video, 26, 200, 201
Virgin Spring, The, 123, 159
visual logic, 50-52, 54-59, 61-64, 108, 113, 125, 187, 210, 212
voiceover, 66, 76, 135, 145, 154-157. *See also* narration
Vu, Bao, 105

W
Welles, Orson, 217
Widmer, Ted, 228
wild sound, 66
Witness, 102-104, 130-134, 137, 187, 214, 223, 224
writers, 216, 230. *See also* screenwriters

Z
Zaka, Zohra, 17
zoom, 93, 94, 96

RICHARD D. PEPPERMAN

Consulting | Editing | Supervision

Consulting | Editing | Supervision

Consulting | Editing | Supervision

Consulting | Editing | Supervision

Consulting | Editing | Supervision

Consulting | Editing | Supervision

Consulting | Editing | Supervision

Consulting | Editing | Supervision

FILM DIRECTING: SHOT BY SHOT

Visualizing from Concept to Screen

Steven D. Katz

Over 160,000 Sold! International best-seller!

Film Directing: Shot by Shot — with its famous blue cover — is the best-known book on directing and a favorite of professional directors as an on-set quick reference guide.

This international bestseller is a complete catalog of visual techniques and their stylistic implications, enabling working filmmakers to expand their knowledge.

Contains in-depth information on shot composition, staging sequences, visualization tools, framing and composition techniques, camera movement, blocking tracking shots, script analysis, and much more.

Includes over 750 storyboards and illustrations, with never-before-published storyboards from Steven Spielberg's *Empire of the Sun*, Orson Welles' *Citizen Kane*, and Alfred Hitchcock's *The Birds*.

"(To become a director) you have to teach yourself what makes movies good and what makes them bad. John Singleton has been my mentor... he's the one who told me what movies to watch and to read *Shot by Shot*."
— Ice Cube, *New York Times*

"A generous number of photos and superb illustrations accompany each concept, many of the graphics being from Katz' own pen... *Film Directing: Shot by Shot* is a feast for the eyes."
— *Videomaker Magazine*

Steven D. Katz is also the author of *Film Directing: Cinematic Motion*.

$27.95 | 366 pages | Order # 7RLS | ISBN: 0-941188-10-8

ORDER FORM

MICHAEL WIESE PRODUCTIONS
11288 VENTURA BLVD., # 621
STUDIO CITY, CA 91604
E-MAIL: MWPSALES@MWP.COM
WEB SITE: WWW.MWP.COM

WRITE OR FAX FOR A FREE CATALOG

PLEASE SEND ME THE FOLLOWING BOOKS:

TITLE	ORDER NUMBER (#RLS _____)	AMOUNT
_____	_____	_____
_____	_____	_____
_____	_____	_____
_____	_____	_____
_____	_____	_____

SHIPPING _____
CALIFORNIA TAX (8.00%) _____
TOTAL ENCLOSED _____

PLEASE MAKE CHECK OR MONEY ORDER PAYABLE TO:

MICHAEL WIESE PRODUCTIONS

(CHECK ONE) ____ MASTERCARD ____ VISA ____ AMEX

CREDIT CARD NUMBER _____

EXPIRATION DATE _____

CARDHOLDER'S NAME _____

CARDHOLDER'S SIGNATURE _____

SHIP TO:

NAME _____

ADDRESS _____

CITY _____ STATE _____ ZIP _____

COUNTRY _____ TELEPHONE _____